# Games on Horseback

### Betty Bennett-Talbot & Steve Bennett

STOREY
BOOKS

*The mission of Storey Communications is to serve our customers
by publishing practical information that encourages personal independence
in harmony with the environment.*

Edited by Marie Salter and Janet Lape
Cover design by Meredith Maker
Cover photograph by Giles Prett/SCI
Text design by Mark Tomasi
Text production by Jen Rork and Erin Lincourt
Photographs by Giles Prett/SCI, unless otherwise indicated
Arena art by Chuck Galey; illustrations on pages
9, 11, 15, 23, 25, 35, 43, 51, 99, and 101 by JoAnna Rissanen-Welch
Indexed by Susan Olason/Indexes & Knowledge Maps

Storey Books are available for special premium and promotional uses and for customized editions. For further information, please call Storey's Custom Publishing Department at 1-800-793-9396.

Printed in Canada by Transcontinental Printing
10 9 8 7 6 5 4 3

**Library of Congress Cataloging-in-Publication Data**

Bennett-Talbot, Betty.
      Games on horseback / Betty Bennett-Talbot, Steven Bennett.
                  p.      cm.
      Includes index.
      ISBN 1-58017-134-6
      1. Games on horseback. I. Bennett, Steven. II. Title.
      SF296.G35 B46 1999
      798—dc21                                                                    98-55400
                                                                                              CIP

# Acknowledgments

I appreciate and acknowledge everyone who has helped this book come to fulfillment, with special gratitude to:

- Lieutenant Colonel Allyn Tidball, who taught me how to teach safety in horse sports, how to direct a school of horsemanship, and how to have fun at polo and drill teams;
- my late husband, John W. Bennett, who made it possible to develop the Hoofbeat Ridge School of Horsemanship and Camp in Wisconsin and who graciously encouraged me to raise, not only our eleven children, but more than a hundred horses;
- my children, who played the games and taught many other children to have fun with horses: Cynthia, Tom, Sally, Steve, Nancy, Jane, Mary, Bill, Dan, Amy, and Molly;
- my husband, John R. Talbot, M.D., who enthusiastically played polo and participated in drills, hunter pace, and competitive distance rides, and developed the Hoofbeat Ridge Ranch in Florida and the Heartland Horse Therapy Program for the Handicapped;
- mentors Chuck Grant, Hilda Gurney, John Bonine, and Doris Bixby Hammett, M.D.;
- Joyce Chartier, for photos, driving, training, and horse care;
- the hundreds of Hoofbeat Ridge horses, who carried the novices and expert riders to new levels of fun while playing games that improve horsemanship skills;
- the Hoofbeat Ridge horses raised in Wisconsin, retired in Florida, especially 33-year-old Misty Morn, who did it all — from polo to distance rides — thanks for the fun!
- Steven John Bennett, who picked up where his father left off, continuing the mission of the Horsemanship Safety Association (HSA): to educate equestrians in safe horsemanship practices.

—*Betty Bennett-Talbot*

© Joyce Chartier

Betty Bennett-Talbot *(left)*,
Steve Bennett *(right)*

# Contents

# Introduction

Games on horseback have long been an equestrian tradition, originating centuries ago by the mounted military. Many of the essential battlefield maneuvers used by medieval knights, Native Americans, and even the British Bengal Lancers contributed to the fun games we now enjoy. For example, the British Bengal Lancers used their lances to unearth the tent pegs in the enemy camp, thus bringing the tent down on the enemy; this tent-pegging technique has since been incorporated into a game that we include in this text, "Litter Control Campaign." Cavalry officers as far back as 600 B.C. played a form of polo in Persia, sometimes using the skulls of their vanquished opponents in place of balls. And the game "Pony Express Relay" on page 64 simulates the dashing, horse-changing ride that characterized the old-time Pony Express.

## Learning Tools for Today's Riders

Games on horseback improve the skill and control of riders, reinforce tactful use of natural aids, offer a diversion for both the rider and the horse — and best of all are fun! Because novice riders are especially concerned about correct seat, use of aids, balance, rhythm, and control, they find it difficult to relax and enjoy the horse during a traditional lesson. By encouraging beginners to tap into their natural riding instincts, games on horseback hasten the progress of new riders while easing the pressure on the horse. Games also change the pace of a lesson, providing stimulating activity to keep riders and horses from becoming bored.

Schooling rides for horses are similar to the classroom experience for people in that they require keen attention and response to the teacher. But just as children and older riders can get bored in equitation lessons, so can horses. Going round and round the ring tends to become monotonous. Horses begin to cut corners or sometimes fall asleep while walking! (Have you ever dozed off while driving a car?) When they're in the pasture, though, horses play naturally. In this same way, they enjoy "playing" with a rider in challenging games.

## The Importance of Safety

In order for games to be fun for riders, horses, and spectators, they must also be safe. Each of the games in this book is designed with the safety of the rider and horse in mind, and this respect for safety should be embraced by everyone who participates

---

### What to Wear

Every sport demands appropriate attire. Designed for the safety and comfort of the horseman, the following should be worn by every rider:

- ASTM-SEI helmet
- Boots or shoes with a 1-inch heel and smooth sole
- Long pants — jeans, breeches, or similar pants

---

◀ Before you can play games on horseback, deck yourself out in appropriate attire: a helmet, boots, and long pants are essential.

in the game. Safety awareness is an attitude or condition that promotes reasonable and prudent action, and it is a ground rule for every game outlined in this book.

Keep in mind that games on horseback can be dangerous when ridden at an uncontrolled speed or when unsupervised by an adult. An experienced rider or adult instructor and assistants should be on hand to referee all games. The instructor or referee is responsible for the safety and education of the riders. Carefully conducted games with rules spelled out and start/finish lines well defined add to the fun. The game's supervisor should take preventive or interventive action to ensure safe procedures, including outlining emergency procedures to all participants and spectators. Yes, spectators can be injured by flying balls, jousting sticks, horses running amuck, or the intense heat of the day.

Striving for excellence and victory is part of the essence of being human, but safety awareness must never be compromised in the heat and excitement of competition. All participants should keep in mind that it is better to allow an opponent to win than to jeopardize the safety of riders and horses. No matter what the prize — a gold cup or a blue ribbon — safety awareness, which prevents accidents and subsequent injury to riders and horses, is the most important aspect of the games.

## The Right Rider for Games

In selecting games for this book, special care was taken to ensure that each game would reinforce or improve riders' horsemanship skills. Because safety requires that riders play games appropriate to their skill level, for each game we have designated the class of rider that has the basic skills needed to participate: Beginning Riders, Intermediate Riders, or Advanced Riders Only.

Whether in a class or riding at home, the best riders for games are those who act responsibly, know their limits, err on the side of safety, and have fun. If a rider has doubts about his or her ability to play a game or wants to play a more challenging game, the instructor should be consulted.

## The Right Horses for Games

Not all horses enjoy close contact games, so instructors should test the game on new horses before using them in a game with novice riders. Many horses need to be introduced gradually to games that involve equipment like balls, whistles, balloons, or polo mallets. The close proximity of horses moving in many directions disturbs some horses, while others welcome the chance to take a "nip" or a kick at a fellow horse. One of our school horses in Wisconsin used to take the opportunity during a game — and sometimes during a lesson — to get even with a bothersome pasturemate while in the ring. Jolly Jo would cross the ring to give Houdini a kick, while the surprised rider struggled to return to the line.

School horses and ranch horses seem to be most suited to games on horseback. Used to moving the cows through dense brush, through canals or streams, and up and down rugged terrain, these courageous Quarter horses spin and adapt to close contact with any animal and take to competitive games almost instantly. Conditions that would spook many a

A well-mannered school horse can be taught to play virtually any game.

pleasure horse seem to be just a day's work for a rancher's horse. We play "cowboy polo" in Florida, and I have yet to see a cow-horse that did not warm quickly to the challenge of polo and other fast close-contact games. Under-the-belly polo shots are no scarier than roping a calf. Of course the best game horses are those trained specifically for the game or competition.

## Conditioning Horses for Games on Horseback

Like people, horses can demonstrate amazing feats of endurance, speed, and agility. They thrill us with their fantastic jumping, racing, roping, spinning, and ballet-like dressage. Some of these movements are quite natural, but others are learned from experienced trainers. In the same way that athletes condition their bodies and minds before competition, horses must be prepared for the physical demands of games on horseback.

All athletes (horse and human) need to warm up and "loosen up" prior to strenuous activity. Most games in this book can be played after a brief warm-up of horse and rider, as is common prior to a typical lesson or trail ride. Riders should recognize and respond to any signs of stress or fatigue in their horses. Riders who are planning to compete in sanctioned shows for speed events, endurance riding, and jumping need to train and condition themselves and their horses well before the competition. Walk/trot preparation coupled with halt/"move on" in a field or ring for at least 1 hour daily will condition a school horse for a riding program within 2 weeks. (Consult the sanctioning body or reference book for an event to obtain needed information on proper conditioning.)

Horses show pleasure when working with kindly, enthusiastic riders. For example, as the rider leans forward urging his mount, the horse feels the excitement, responding with a spirited display of energy. That's a happy horse!

Remember to recognize the horses' physical and mental limits, and don't let riders push them beyond. Riders should know that taking care of the horses' needs, such as wiping them down or bathing them after an event, is part of playing the games. Encourage riders to praise horses well for the good game; the horses will reward them by their willingness to play again.

## Sportsmanship

Good sportsmanship, courtesy, and respect play an important role in competitive sports. If played safely and under supervision, games on horseback can be a good way for riders to learn cooperation, team spirit, and synchronization. For a successful game, behavior must be respectful, even though competitors may be fired with determination to beat their opponents. Riders must assess every action for the potential risk to horse or rider. While problems may occur because of equipment failure, more often they're caused by inexperience, insufficient preparation, insufficient conditioning, or even lack of knowledge or respect for the rules.

## General Guidelines

Many of the games in this book are traditional games on horseback that have been played for years by horsemen and mounted warriors. Some have been modified to enhance riding skills or to eliminate safety hazards. The games most often involve a standard group of eight riders, an instructor, and an assistant. We have found the use of "dressage letters" to be quite helpful when providing directions and designating start/finish lines during games and in riding lessons. With eight horses and riders in a riding ring, the "rules of the road" must be followed to ensure the safety of all. Here are the basics:

▸ A safe ratio is one instructor for four riders.
▸ Maintain one horse-length distance from all other horses. Exceptions include pairs events, drill team, or games requiring close contact, such as Polo and Stick Relay.
▸ No passing — avoid trapping a horse between the rail and your horse. If getting too close to the horse in front of you, cross the ring, circle with your horse, or slow down.

- Ride in the same direction — track left (walk toward any fence or wall and turn left) or track right.
- To avoid confusion or collision, use the "command of preparation" so that all riders perform the same movement at the same time. For example, to initiate a group jog (or trot), the instructor says, "Prepare to jog," then pauses for 2 to 5 seconds and says, "And jog," with emphasis on the word "jog," meaning "now."
- Use "parking places" in the center of the arena to start and end game times or to make tack adjustments or changes. The arena is similar to a racetrack, with the "track" being the outer edge near the fence or wall and the "pit stop" area within the confines of the track. Horses are lined up side by side (safely spaced) in the center (along a line from point A to point C), facing one side of the arena.

## How to Use This Book

It is the authors' hope that this book of games will provide hours of good, safe fun for riders of all ages and abilities. Presented in a simplified, two-page format for quick reference and use in the arena, each game in this book serves as an introduction to many exciting competitive events in the horse world, including Western rodeo speed events, long distance riding, jumping, polo, and drill team. Instructors should familiarize riders with the game prior to mounting.

While these games are presented in a format for groups of eight riders, many games can be played with only one horse. Each section begins with a general introduction and a list of special equipment that all good riders need to be safe. (See Safety Tips box.)

Minimum rider levels are indicated for each game, followed by a brief description, the game's purpose, instructions, cautions, variations, and tips. Riders with disabilities, Special Olympians, and others can adapt many of these games for use in their programs.

May these games help you share the joy of horses, ride well, and work with others in happy cooperation.

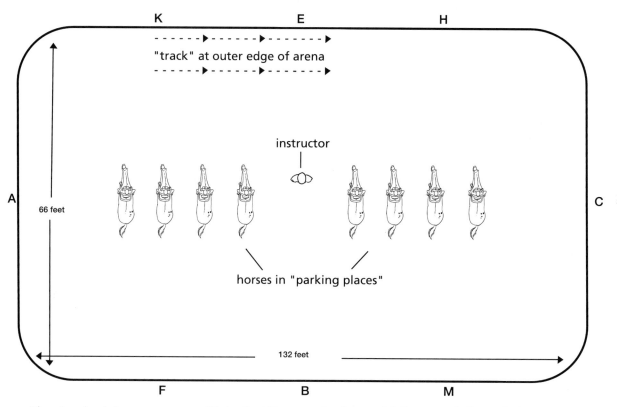

The standard dressage arena. (Note that if general safety guidelines are followed, the games in this book be played in any size arena.) An instructor should observe all games.

## Safety Tips for Games on Horseback

Most horses are bigger, stronger, and faster than people. Therefore, the potential for injury in horseback riding is great if we fail to use common sense and take reasonable precautions. Here are some points to keep in mind:

• *Always* **wear an ASTM- or SEI-approved helmet with chin strap fastened** when mounted and whenever around horses.

• *Always* **wear shoes or boots with a relatively smooth sole and at least a 1" heel** to help keep feet from sliding through the stirrups.

• *Always* **wear clothes that fit,** *not* baggy, loose clothes or jewelry that might get caught on tack or manes; also avoid earrings that may get caught in the helmet harness.

• **Learn the emergency dismount** before you get on a horse, and practice it until it becomes automatic. You may need it someday. (See "Squirrel" on page 8.)

• *Always* **be alert.** Keep your eyes on your horse, and know what he is doing at all times.

• **Keep at least one horse-length from other horses** while riding, when possible. When riding behind another horse, look between your horse's ears — you should be able to see the hind feet of the horse in front of you.

• **Introduce your horse to new play equipment** (e.g., balls, sticks, cones, etc.) *before* the game, so he won't spook or jump. Let him look at the equipment and see how it will be moved and used.

• **Check your girth or cinch** just before mounting, after mounting, and at least once per hour.

• **Tie your horse** with halter and rope (*never* reins) to a post or tree (*never* fence boards).

• **Know your horse's limits.** Learn your horse's vital signs and how to measure for pulse, respiration, and temperature, so you'll have a good idea how he's feeling. (Pulse averages 40 beats per minute, respiration 8 to 12 breaths per minute, and temperatures 99 to 101°F.)

• *Don't* **ride alone.** It's more fun and safest to ride with friends or at the very least with someone watching you. If you head out on the trail, be sure to tell someone where you're going, what you're going to do, when you'll be back, and who to call if you need help.

• *Never* **ride double.** Like bicycles, horses are built for one rider at a time. In an emergency, you need to dismount quickly, which is not possible with two riders.

• *Never* **tie yourself to a horse.** Always be able to get away in 3 seconds or less.

• *Don't* **fool around.** Leave horseplay to horses.

• *Don't* **hand-feed horses.** Horses can't see their mouths and might accidentally nibble a hand or finger. Use a special "treats" bucket instead.

• *Don't* **chew gum or candy while riding.** One bad bounce could cause you to choke.

• *Don't* **stand in a horse's blind spot** (directly in front of or behind him) or block his natural escape route (straight ahead).

• *Don't* **ride in an area with loose horses;** they may make trouble.

• *Don't* **clean a stall with a horse in it;** you may accidentally poke your horse with a tool and get pinned against a wall, kicked, or stepped on.

# I

# Basic Group Games

Games on horseback derive from many sources, some from our Native American forebears. The basic games in this section are intended for first-time riders. These fun, challenging games are designed to improve elementary horse handling and maneuvering skills and to add variety to what otherwise might seem repetitive riding practice.

Each game has as many variations as you can devise. A small riding area can be used for as few as two participants or, for more expansive games, use open rangeland and woods and involve many groups of riders. These basic games imitate hunting techniques used by Native Americans and simulate their quiet, stealthy technique of stalking animals.

Becoming one with the horse — riding in well-balanced harmony with the horse's movements — is the desired result of these games.

Requiring riders to follow, guess, and make independent decisions, these basic games are meant to be educational rather than competitive. Squirrel and Around the World are important basic games, particularly for beginning riders. Most of all, we want the riders to enjoy their horses and to consider them willing partners in the games. Other riders and spectators contribute to the spirit of fun.

Good reliable school horses are best for these and all other games on horseback.

## Equipment Needed for Games

- Logs
- Hay bales
- Poles
- Barrels (55-gallon [250-liter] drums)

- Slips of paper
- "Treasure" for Treasure Hunt (e.g., apple, crackers, etc.)

◀ Follow the Leader is a great game for beginning riders. The instructor or the leader determines gait, pattern, and level of difficulty.

# 1 Squirrel

▶ Beginning Riders

We believe that riders should learn how to get off their horse in an emergency *before* their first riding experience. The emergency dismount, or Squirrel, is part of the "pre-ride" demonstration given by many good riding schools when showing students how to mount, start, halt, and rein a horse. This is the first type of dismount taught to our students and the one we use for the first several lessons. It is perhaps one of the most important skills riders learn. When the Squirrel is done properly, the rider lands feet first, unencumbered by reins and stirrups. Though here the maneuver is treated as a game, students should know that this dismount may save their life.

**Note:** The commands for each movement are given in parentheses.

- Take feet out of stirrups. ("Feet.")
- Drop reins on horse's neck. ("Reins.")
- Place hands on saddle swells or horse's neck or withers. ("Hands.")

- Swing both legs back and right leg up over horse's rump while leaning forward; push off horse with hands to vault off. Bend knees to absorb shock when landing. ("Vault.")
- Lift reins over horse's head and hold horse in ready-to-lead position.

## Instructions

1. Students are in "parking places" in center of ring. Assistants hold horse.
2. Instructor demonstrates and explains the squirreling sequence.
3. Instructor calls out key words in sequence, and students perform each step.
4. Students remount and squirrel at instructor's command.
- **Winner:** The first person safely off and standing next to the horse, holding reins.

## Cautions

- Initially, students should perform one at a time, as instructor talks them through steps.
- Instructor or assistant should stand nearby to spot student, if necessary.
- Be sure students perform steps in order.
- Be clear in instructions.
- Make sure students drop stirrups and reins before dismount.
- Advise students to bend knees to absorb shock when landing.
- Horses should stand quietly or stop (if moving) when student vaults off.

## Variations

- Make it a race once students can perform well. First student to dismount, take reins over horse's head, and stand in leading (or ready-to-lead) position wins.
- When able, have students squirrel from a walk, then a trot.

## Tips

- Have students practice swinging legs back and forth, with hands on the front of the saddle.
- Tell students that their goal is to swing themselves up out of the saddle.
- To instill confidence, have students practice one at a time on a small bareback horse or pony.
- Ground exercise for leg swing: Stand on one leg, extend arms forward and reach to touch ground; when reaching forward extend other leg straight out behind. Return to upright position, and do same with opposite leg.

When Squirrel is done well, the dismount appears to be one fluid movement.

# 2 Around the World

▶ **Beginning Riders**

Remember learning how to ride a bicycle and how difficult it was to find your balance? In this game, riders learn where the balance points are on the back of the horse and in their own seat. They have to actively use their weight, arms, and legs to lift, shift, and pivot to get all the way around in the saddle. Good riders can do this without using their hands!

### PURPOSE

Encourages riders to rely primarily on their seat for balance, the ideal in good horsemanship. Increased confidence and the ability to balance with the seat frees the rider to use hands, legs, and weight shifts as aids in moving the horse.

# Instructions

1. Riders are mounted and in center of ring in "parking place."
2. Instructor gives signal to begin.
3. Riders drop reins, remove both feet from stirrups, then swing right leg over horse's neck to sit sideways on horse's near side.

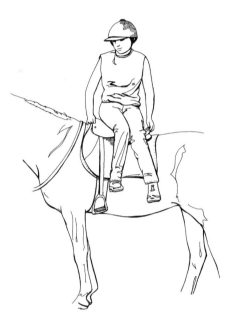

4. Riders swing left leg over horse's croup (rump) to sit backward on horse.

5. Riders swing right leg over croup to sit sideways on horse's far side.

6. Riders swing left leg over horse's neck to return to the correct position, then place feet back in stirrups.

▶ **Winner:** First rider with feet back in the stirrups.

# Cautions

▶ Horses should be in their "parking places."
▶ On rider's first try, instructor holds horse at reins to assure rider horse will stay "parked" and in case rider slips off saddle.
▶ Riders should be careful not to kick the horse.

# Variation

Have riders go Around the World clockwise so they become comfortable with both directions.

# 3 Follow the Leader

▶ **Beginning Riders**

Young Indian braves learned how to hunt by following, observing, and imitating the movements of an elder who searched for and stalked prey. Follow the Leader derives from that tradition and is a great game for beginning riders. It allows many riders to take a turn as "leader," instilling confidence in the process. The pattern to be followed must be one that all riders can follow. This game doesn't have a winner or loser; it's meant for fun. Pick up the pace, add some obstacles, and this game will challenge even the best riders.

# Instructions

1. Instructor chooses a leader who can perform the desired movements.
2. Riders line up one horse-length behind the leader.
3. Instructor allows designated leader to establish a pattern at a gait appropriate for the class or directs leader through a pattern.
4. Riders try to follow the leader, always maintaining a distance of one horse-length between riders.
5. Instructor signals for leaders to change at the end of a prescribed pattern or after an established time limit. The new leader can be the next person in line or the rider who best followed the pattern.

# Cautions

▸ The instructor must supervise closely and limit patterns and actions to those that all riders in the group can perform.

▸ Remember: Safety first! Leaders may get silly and create unsafe patterns.
▸ For safety, have riders perform difficult patterns one at a time.
▸ Do not use lope or canter.

# Variations

▸ Pattern can include equitation exercises (e.g., arm circles; foot rotation without stirrups; touching poll, stirrup, tail, and so on) in "parking places" as a warm-up or for small or unsure riders.
▸ The instructor can call out a pattern for riders to perform.
▸ For intermediate or advanced riders, include appropriate obstacles as shown below (e.g., jumps for jumpers).

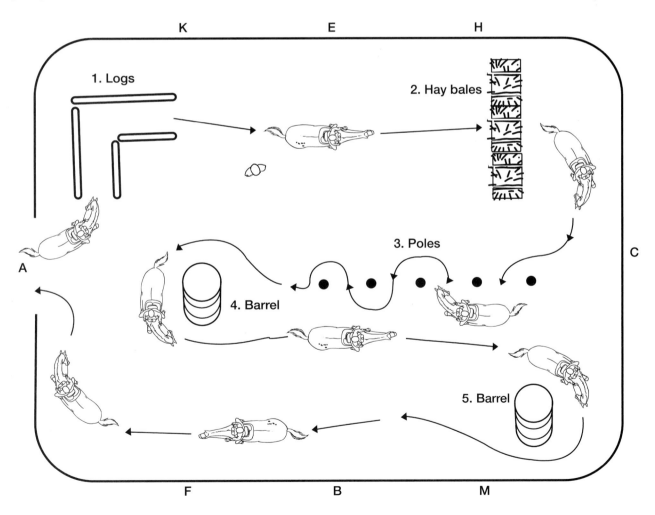

# 4 Charades

▶ **Beginning Riders**

Charades has Native American roots. When close to game they were stalking, Native Americans used hand signals and gestures to communicate within the hunting party so as not to make noise and scare off their prey. Charades is a good resting game after an active class. It can also be a great rainy-day unmounted game.

As is common in parlor charades, players are assigned items to act out. See the suggestion box on the next page for ideas. Write items out on slips of paper, place in a hat, and let the fun begin!

**PURPOSE**

Reinforces knowledge of horse anatomy, tack, gaits, and movements.

# Instructions

1. Riders divide into two teams.
2. If mounted, riders and horses are in "parking places."
3. One rider from a team takes a slip of paper from hat and rides to the front of the class. Using gestures without speaking, rider acts out item.
4. Other riders guess what is being portrayed.
▶ **Winner:** First person to guess what rider is acting out.

## Suggestions

- Tack: Parts of saddle and bridle, saddle pad, hoofpick, halter, lead rope
- Rider movements: Mounting, dismounting, jumping position
- Commands: Halt, walk, trot, canter, turn left/right
- Horse gaits: Footfalls at each gait
- Styles/types of riding: English, Western, dressage, jumping
- Horses at your barn
- Horse people: Riders, actors, instructors, farrier, veterinarian
- Tools for grooming, stable care

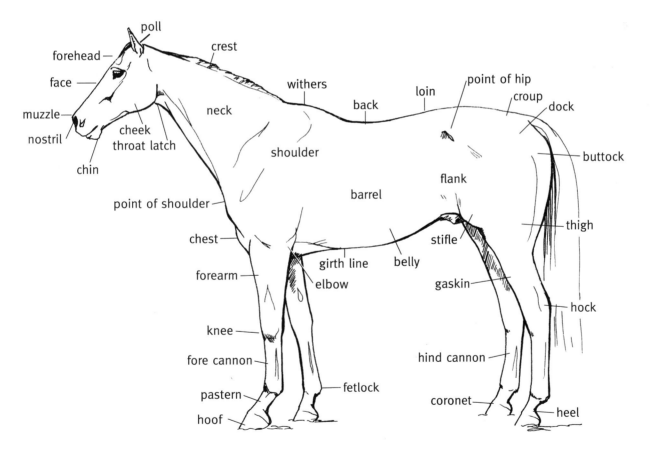

It takes a clever player to act out parts of the horse's anatomy; but if done well, it's sure to be something participants never forget.

# 5 Treasure Hunt

▶ **Beginning Riders**

An individual or team event that can be timed to make it more challenging, Treasure Hunt is an outgrowth of Native Americans' and pioneers' need to find water, food, and shelter. It can be played in the ring with beginning riders or in an open area with more skillful riders. Items are placed on barrels, in buckets, or on fence posts throughout the ring. Riders are equipped with a list of items to retrieve and a small pouch or bag to carry or to attach to the saddle. Then the fun begins! An unexpected challenge arises when horses try to help themselves to certain horse "necessities" such as apples or carrots.

**PURPOSE**

Challenges riders to ride independently in many directions, reining and maneuvering close to objects, and can include mounting/dismounting practice.

# Instructions

1. Prior to game, instructor places items for riders to collect at various stations around the ring. For beginning riders, items should be easily accessible from the saddle. To maintain the traditional theme, use items that would be valuable on a long journey to the unsettled West. Try an apple, carrot, egg, vegetable, piece of twine, cup of water, wrapped crackers, pine cone, small stuffed animal, beef jerky, alfalfa cube, and so on. (Be sure food items are in sealed wrappers.)
2. Riders start and finish in "parking places" in the center of the ring.
3. Instructor gives riders a list of hidden items and a plastic bag or pouch to hang from the saddle.
4. On command, riders proceed at a walk, individually or in pairs, to gather items.
▸ **Winner:** Rider or team to find all items and return to starting places.

# Cautions

▸ Watch horse interactions and spacing in the ring. Horses should be no closer than one horse-length apart.
▸ Provide adequate supervision.
▸ For large open-area treasure hunts, designate pairs or teams so no one rides alone.
▸ Limit team size to no more than eight riders.
▸ Do not allow hand-feeding. Put treats for horses on the ground or in a "treat bucket."

# Tips

▸ To avoid congestion at stations, allow only one rider at a time to take an item.
▸ Provide food items in sealed wrappers (e.g., wrapped crackers, jerky sticks).
▸ Be sure all horses are accustomed to noises of objects, such as plastic bags.
▸ Western saddles work best for hanging a bag or sack.

▸ Include a map and field guide (pictures of items) for open-area hunts.
▸ After the game, when horses are untacked, allow riders to treat their horses with one or more food items.
▸ Put the list in a plastic bag or sleeve and tie it to the saddle with baling twine.
▸ In large team events, have riders wear different colored pinnies or helmet covers to identify each team.
▸ Indicate limit of territory where items may be found. Clues to hiding places may be included on list.

# Variations

▸ Place items in such a way that riders are forced to dismount and remount.
▸ Hide items from view in an enclosed field.
▸ Choose items naturally occurring in the area — leaves from certain trees, birch bark, wild fruit or berries, moss, feathers, mushrooms. (Beware of poisonous leaves, plants, and berries.)
▸ Allow a faster pace, such as a trot/jog or canter/lope.
▸ Have a "picnic treasure hunt." Have riders find their lunch!
▸ Tailor the search to match the season: Easter eggs, American flags, small Halloween pumpkins, and Christmas ornaments are just a few items that can make this game more festive and fun.

### SUGGESTED TREASURES

- Food items: Apple, carrot, wrapped snacks
- Clothing: Gloves, jacket
- Equipment: Crop, brush for grooming
- Anything riders most want — stuffed animals, sports cards.

# II

# Elimination Games

With horses, we can continue to enjoy many of the popular games we played as kids. Who hasn't played Simon Says, Musical Chairs, or tried to keep an egg on a spoon? While reinforcing riding skills, these games help new riders to relax and lose themselves in a focused activity. Many riders say, "I can't get him to do it"; some try too hard to perform a skill but discover themselves able to perform that same skill successfully during a game.

With the exception of the musical games, as few as two participants are necessary to play the games in this section. Minimal equipment is needed and, as before, variations are limited only by your imagination. Beginning riders should move slowly, but advanced riders can increase the speed and complexity of the games and devise extremely challenging versions. The best horse for this game is one that likes to play and is tuned into the rider. As with all games, horses should be tolerant of the rider and equipment used. Horses should be "introduced" (walked or ridden up) to each piece of equipment prior to the game.

## Equipment Needed for Games

- Eggs
- Large spoons
- Dollar bills, play money, slips of paper
- Crepe-paper ribbon
- Cavalletti
- Burlap sacks
- Radio or cassette/CD player
- Knit hats, helmet covers, paper hats

◀ The Egg 'n' Spoon Race is a fun, challenging game for individual riders and for pairs, as shown here.

19

# 6 Simon Says

▶ **Beginning Riders**

A great game for new riders, Simon Says helps build rider confidence and relieves the initial anxiety experienced by many. In this game, riders are encouraged to stand, stetch, bend, and twist while in the saddle, thus improving their balance, security, and confidence on their horse. Riders quickly discover that they can move around quite a bit without fear of falling.

**PURPOSE**

Helps rider learn horse anatomy and reinforces stretching and balancing exercises that are often done at the start of a lesson. Encourages rider to be attentive and alert to instructor's voice and commands.

# Instructions

1. As game begins, rider should be mounted, in "parking places," or proceeding at the walk, single file along the track. (Remember to maintain at least one horse-length between horses.)
2. If riders are on track, instructor tells them to ride at a specific gait, execute a certain movement, or touch the horse in a particular spot. Some commands begin with "Simon says"; some do not.
3. Riders follow command when it's prefaced by the words "Simon says." A rider who follows a command without the preface is eliminated.
▸ **Winner:** Rider(s) remaining in game after series of commands are given.

# Cautions

▸ Before giving a command, make sure that all players are able to perform the movement at the gait they're moving.
▸ Beginning riders should play while their horse is halted or in "parking place."
▸ Use common sense. Be careful not to jeopardize riders' safety to get a single winner; it's far better to have several winners than to have a rider on the ground.

# Variations

▸ Replace "Simon" with the instructor's name, for example "Joe says."
▸ Increase the level of difficulty by speeding up the sequence of movements.

Here are some simple commands to get you started:
• Simon says, "Touch poll."
• Simon says, "Drop left stirrup."
• Simon says, "Trot."
• Simon says, "Reverse."
• Simon says, "Halt."

Simon Says is great fun for little ones, offering them lots of opportunity to succeed.

# 7

# Egg 'n' Spoon Race

▶ **Beginning Riders**

In this traditional game, the riders hold a small round object, such as an egg (hard-boiled or uncooked), pine cone, or small apple, in a large spoon as they ride. The goal is to ride at the specified gait without dropping the object. Riders may not touch the object once the game begins.

### PURPOSE

Teaches quiet hands — essential for good horse-rider communication; requires focused attention and concentration.

# Instructions

1. Riders start in "parking places" or along track in single line and halted.
2. Riders are handed egg and spoon.
3. Instructor directs riders to perform various movements at a specific gait, reining their horses with one hand while keeping the object balanced in the spoon with the other.
4. If and when the object falls, rider and horse leave the game and "park" in the center of the ring.
- **Winner:** Last rider(s) to carry object in spoon.

# Cautions

- Be sure all riders can rein with one hand. As with other games, safety takes priority over having a single winner.
- Be sure all horses rein well and can be ridden with one hand.

# Variations

- A variety of objects and "spoons" can be used (e.g., tennis racket). Be creative.
- For better riders, add speed and complexity by using a timed course or an obstacle course.

Playing the game in pairs, as here, requires that riders maintain the same gait.

The challenge, of course, is to keep the egg from rolling out of the spoon. Keep your hand steady!

# 8

# Ride-a-Buck

▶ **B e g i n n i n g   R i d e r s**

Ride-a-Buck is another classic game on horseback; it works especially well with a large class. The goal is for the rider to keep a dollar bill between seat and saddle while riding. Need a prize? Let the winner keep the buck. Or, if you're feeling especially generous, let the winner keep all the bucks!

# Instructions

1. Riders begin in "parking places" or in single file. (Remember to maintain at least one horse-length between riders.)
2. Instructor helps place "buck" (play money works well) under rider's seat, elbow, calf, or ball of foot, so half of dollar bill is visible.
3. Instructor asks riders to perform various movements without touching dollar bill. Riders execute moves as requested, trying to keep dollar bill in place without using their hands.

▶ **Winner:** Last rider to have dollar bill in place.

# Cautions

▶ Some horses may jump or become skittish when the dollar bill flutters away; check horses for sensitivity before class.
▶ Make sure the dollar placement helps to stabilize and improve rider balance and skill. For riders new to this game, careful instructions as to proper dollar placement can help.

# Variations

▶ Riders new to this game do well riding bareback.
▶ Place the dollar in different locations to add variety.
▶ Instead of a dollar bill, use play money or paper of different sizes.
▶ Challenge riders with progressively difficult movements and patterns. Have students maneuver around poles or barrels.

Place dollar bills in several locations to improve seat and challenge the best riders.

# 9

# Ribbon Race

▶ Intermediate Riders

One of the most popular games to play with a large group, Ribbon Race requires that each of a pair of riders hold one end of a 3-foot (.9-m) length of crepe-paper ribbon between them as they ride side by side. When the riders separate and the ribbon stretches beyond its limit and breaks, or if one rider drops the ribbon, the pair is eliminated. Both spectators and participants enjoy this challenging game, as riders reach and lean to keep their ribbon intact while simultaneously trying to keep their horses in sync. The best teams are those able to ride "boot to boot" while doing stops, turns, and changing gaits.

### PURPOSE

Improves ability to direct and control the horse, while at the same time co-ordinating riding with a partner. Teaches teamwork and is an excellent training game for drill team candidates, as riders must maintain same speed and gait.

# Instructions

1. Riders break into paired teams, or instructor establishes teams based on compatibility of horses.
2. Riders pair up with their partners and practice riding side by side at the walk once around the ring.
3. Instructor hands each team a 3-foot (.9-m) length of crepe-paper ribbon.
4. Each team member holds one end of the ribbon, while riding at instructor's direction.
5. Instructor calls out commands, starting with walk and halt, and adding turns and faster gaits if needed.

# Cautions

- Instructor and riders must watch for and respond to horse body language and threatening gestures, as teams will be riding close together.
- Be sure to pair horses that get along well together. Promptly change horse combinations that don't work.
- Maintain one horse-length between teams of riders, and stay clear of other teams.

- Pairs should be careful to allow extra space and not to "hug the fence."
- Instructor must use command of preparation to cue all riders at once (e.g., "Prepare to . . .").

# Variations

- Shorten the ribbons to 2 feet (.6 m).
- Have riders hold end of ribbon under leg, as in Ride-a-Buck.
- Make teams of three riders using two ribbons — a real challenge!
- Have a bareback ribbon race.

# Tips

- Riders should talk to each other to synchronize movements.
- To maintain comfortable distance during turns, rider to inside of ring must ride slower than rider to outside of ring.
- Teams should designate one partner to lead and one to follow.

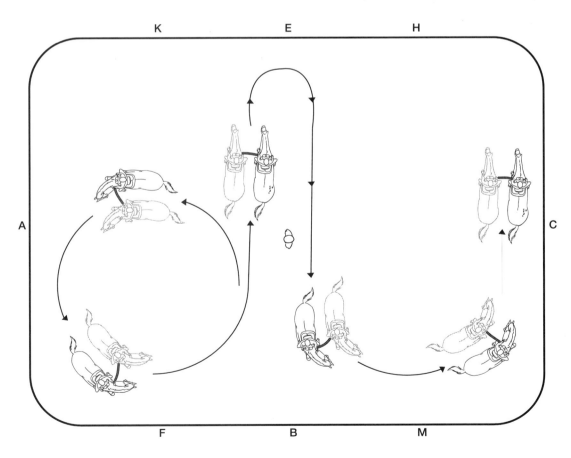

# 10

# Musical Stalls

▶ **Intermediate Riders**

Similar in approach to musical chairs, Musical Stalls is a game in which riders race to 4- by 4-foot (1.2- by 1.2-meter) "stalls" made from cavalletti or poles when the music stops. Because there is always one fewer stall than there are players, one rider is eliminated in each round. For safety, these rules must be followed by all participants: No crossing through the center of the arena, and no turning to ride in the opposite direction. In addition, if the horse steps out of the stall over the rail, rider and horse are eliminated.

# Instructions

1. In the center of the ring, set up "stalls" defined by cavalletti or poles; make sure there is one fewer stall than the number of riders.
2. Riders walk along the fence while "stalls" are being constructed.
3. Instructor plays music or signals spectators to sing — a cooperative crowd is needed for the latter! Riders circle arena at designated gait.
4. After a minute or two, instructor turns off music or signals spectators to stop singing; riders ride into nearest stall and remain there. Rider left without a stall is eliminated.
5. One stall is removed, and instructor repeats music cycle.
▶ **Winner:** Rider to get to stall in last round of game.

# Cautions

▶ Avoid racing or running to stalls; riders must maintain a constant gait.
▶ Be alert to crowding horses, and watch ears for signs of trouble. Ears that are pinned back flat against the horse's head are a clear sign of stress.
▶ Riders must always move forward to a stall, not reverse direction.

# Variations

▶ Substitute burlap sacks for stalls. Horse must have one foot on a sack when the music stops.
▶ Have riders dismount and lead horse to stall or sack when music stops.
▶ For final two riders, have a race (at designated gait) from one end of the ring to the stall at the other end.
▶ Substitute trees for posts if playing game in the open.

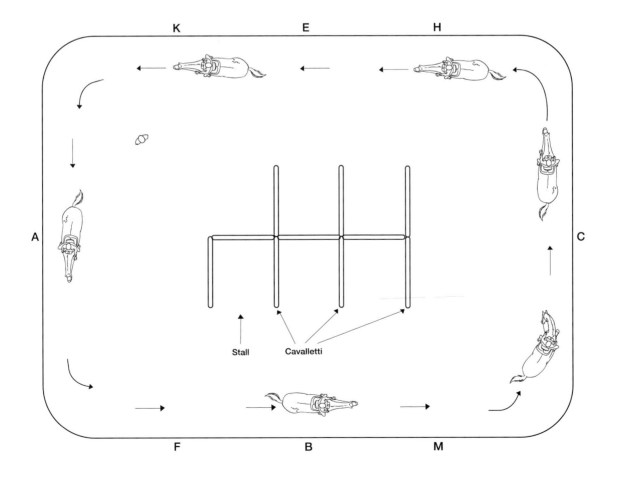

# 11 Musical Mount

▶ **Intermediate Riders**

This fun, quick game teaches riders to mount and dismount a horse from either side and teaches the horse to accommodate a rider without fear. No props are needed other than the instructor's voice or a couple of vocal kids on the sidelines. The riders may moan and groan about mounting on the off side, but they'll soon warm to the challenge and enjoy it!

<table>
<tr><td>PURPOSE</td></tr>
<tr><td>Teaches rider flexibility in mounting; teaches horse to accept mount from off side. Also teaches riders to mount and dismount quickly.</td></tr>
</table>

# Instructions

1. Entire game takes place in "parking places" in center of ring.
2. Mounted riders line up side by side in center of ring, with at least one horse-length between horses.
3. Instructor designates side from which to dismount (i.e., "near" or "off") and side on which to remount.
4. Instructor starts music or signals spectators to sing — a cooperative crowd is needed for the latter!
5. After a minute or two, instructor turns off music or signals spectators to stop singing.
6. Riders dismount and remount as instructed. Last rider up is eliminated from game.
7. Instructor designates mount/dismount sides and starts and stops music again.
8. Riders are eliminated for dismounting or mounting from wrong side; it may help to remind riders at the start of the music from which side they will dismount.
- **Winner:** First rider to mount from designated side in last round of game.

# Cautions

▸ Horses should be accustomed to off-side mount and dismount prior to game.

▸ Riders must all be able to mount unassisted, unless all have assistants.

▸ Riders should do "squirrel" (emergency) dismount. (See page 8.) Remind riders to remove feet from stirrups and drop reins before jumping off.

▸ Allow plenty of room between horses so that riders do not collide.

▸ Riders should *never* walk behind horses — only in front.

# Variations

▸ Easiest: Dismount/remount from near side (horse's left).

▸ Hard: Dismount off side, remount near side.

▸ Harder: Dismount near side, remount off side.

▸ Hardest: Dismount/remount off side.

▸ Bareback version is especially challenging.

▸ With limited time, winner is the first person to remount; this allows all riders to play many games.

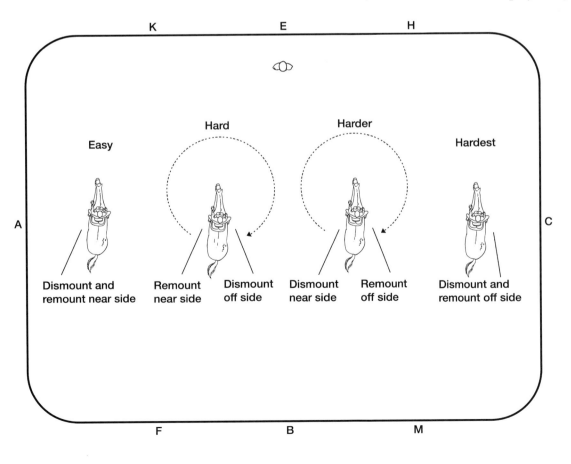

# 12 Musical Pairs

▶ **Intermediate Riders**

This is a good game to play when there are lots of students and not enough room for all their horses. Because this game assigns two riders to each horse, it can be played in a small space — indoors on a rainy day, for instance.

Choose your favorite music, and let the fun begin! Musical Pairs can be played to country, jazz, classical, rock 'n' roll, even rap. Bring lots of music, and let the winning team choose the next song.

> **PURPOSE**
>
> Encourages teamwork; students learn "leg-up" mounting procedure and how to help another person mount. Riders also learn how to move horse quickly within the same gait.

# Instructions

1. Riders divide into pairs; each pair of riders teams up with one horse.
2. One rider gives partner "leg-up" mount on horse.
3. Riders form a large circle in outer part of ring; unmounted players stand in a small circle at center of ring.
4. Instructor announces gait for game and starts music.
5. Mounted riders circle ring to the left (counter-clockwise).
6. Instructor stops music.
7. Riders ride to partner, dismount, and help partner mount. Last team to remount is eliminated.
8. Instructor repeats music cycle; team members continue to alternate standing in small circle or riding around arena.
   - **Winner:** First team to remount in last round of game.

# Cautions

- When giving "leg-up," use proper lifting technique: Keep back straight, bend knees, and lift with legs.
- Pair riders who can assist one another with mounting.
- Be sure riders maintain proper spacing (one horse-length all around the horse).

> ### Leg-up Mount
>
> Rider gathers reins of horse in left hand at withers and on right side of saddle seat. Rider bends left leg at knee, keeping the thigh straight to the hip and the shin perpendicular to ground. Assistant bends her knees and grabs rider's left knee in left hand, shin in right hand. Rider *bounces* off right leg and on a count of three, rider jumps from right leg while assistant gives "boost," holding left leg and rider up into the saddle. Important! The main thrust of energy comes from the rider's bounce.

- Riders cannot cut across the ring or change directions.
- Heavy riders may need a mounting block or capable assistant to help them mount.
- If allowing faster gaits, be sure riders don't run over partners.
- Remind partners standing in the small circle not to move toward their mounted partner but to remain in their own spot. Have them stand on a sack or small rug as a reminder!

# Variations

- If riders are unable to help one another mount, have partner remain dismounted.
- This can be a great bareback game, especially in winter!
- Require riders to dismount and lead horse to partner when music stops.

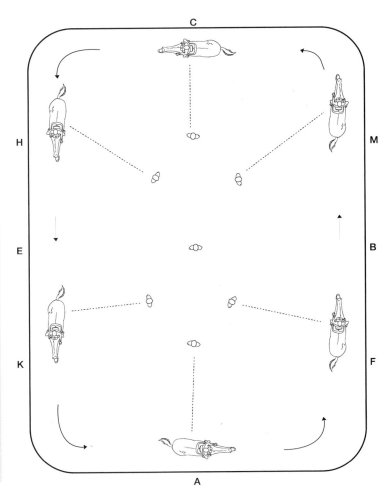

# 13 Hat Snatch

▶ A d v a n c e d   R i d e r s   O n l y

In Hat Snatch, the riders wear knit hats, helmet covers, or homemade paper hats over their regular helmets. At the "Go" signal, riders attempt to snatch hats off each other's heads. The last rider wearing a hat wins.

Similar in some ways to the childhood game of "keep away," keeping a hat on your head can be just as challenging as snatching one, or two, or three. . . . Good luck!

> **PURPOSE**
>
> Mostly just for fun! Improves rider's ability to maneuver and manage horse and to outmaneuver other riders; a great "let loose" game.

# Instructions

1. Riders place knit hats, helmet covers, or home-made paper hats over their helmets and spread out in ring.
2. Instructor signals for game to begin.
3. Riders move toward other riders and attempt to take each other's hats.
4. Riders hand hats to instructor or deposit hats in buckets set out throughout the ring.
   - **Winner:** Last rider with hat on head.

# Cautions

- Horses should be accustomed to being near each other in close proximity, as in drill team.
- Avoid excessive speed and close proximity to rear of horse.
- Allow walk or trot only.
- Be sure all horses get along with one another — no kickers!
- Caution riders not to approach one another from the rear. Approach from the side.
- Don't let riders pin others against the fence.

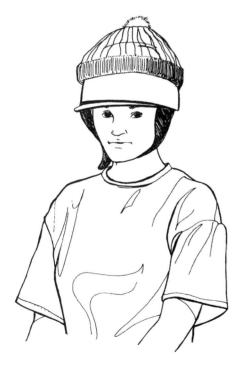

Hats that "give," such as a knit hat, work best for this fun, "let loose" game.

# Variations

- Makes a fun team event with two or more teams; each team wears the same color hat or shirt.
- Instead of hats, use bandanas tucked in pants, balloons on backs (be careful — horses must be conditioned to the sound of popping balloons), or ribbons on one or both legs. As always, be sure to introduce horses to props or equipment *before* the game starts.

The bigger the hat, the more there is to snatch!

# III

# Basic Races

It's off to the races! In most sports, competition challenges and improves the skills of participants. The same is true in horseback riding. These basic races excite riders. A race doesn't have to be run at a full gallop to be thrilling — just getting and staying ahead of the competition is enough for many riders. And virtually any activity can be made into a race, from the "Squirrel" emergency dismount (see Basic Group Games in the first section) to driving pony carts.

Most of the games in this section require nothing more than horses, tack, dressage letters, and perhaps a few 55-gallon (250-liter) drums. Tennis Tournament requires a few rackets and old balls; you also will need two ponies and two carts for that race. Saddle-Up Race, Rescue Race, and Pony Cart Race are team events that can be played with just two pairs of riders and with only two horses. Tortoise and Hare Race, and Red Light, Green Light are two favorites of beginning riders, emphasizing basic start/halt/rein skills. Modifying any of the games will challenge even the best riders. Riders who think they're "pretty good," will find the "No Hands" Contest and Sidesaddle Race a particular challenge to their riding skill and balance, respectively.

As always, you will want to use good reliable horses that enjoy variety and are responsive to the rider. A speedy horse that doesn't respond quickly to rider commands will often be beaten by a slower, more responsive horse. The ideal game horse is the one that tries to anticipate the rider's desires. Smart game players also are quick to pick a horse that knows the game well.

## Equipment Needed for Games

- Tarp
- Tennis rackets
- Tennis balls
- Buckets
- Ponies or minihorses
- Pony carts

- Cones
- Peacock or other safety stirrups
- Crepe-paper ribbon
- Barrels (55-gallon [250-liter] drums)
- Jump standards

◀ A good start is important in games on horseback. For a group start, horses should be in a straight line and at least one horse-length apart, as shown here.

37

# 14 Tortoise and Hare Race

▶ **Beginning Riders**

Because this game can be played either slow or fast at any gait, it challenges *all* levels of riders and is one of the best games for beginning riders. In the Tortoise Race, the person who rides slowest without stopping wins. In the Hare Race, the fastest rider wins. The instructor sets the gait — walk or trot (jog) — and riders must maintain that gait to win.

**PURPOSE**

Improves rider's ability to move horse slower and faster within each gait using gentle aids (e.g., nudges with seat, light half-halt with hands, gentle squeeze with legs) and is a great equalizer in classes for students with different riding skills. Tremendously helpful to students learning light, subtle use of aids.

# Instructions for Tortoise Race

1. Riders line up at start line.
2. Instructor signals start.
3. Riders must ride a straight line and not weave.
▶ **Winner:** Last rider to cross finish line without stopping.

# Instructions for Hare Race

1. Riders line up side by side behind start line.
2. Instructor announces gait and signals start.
3. After you cross the finish line, turn left and line up between H and M.
▶ **Winner:** First rider to cross finish line at established gait.

# Cautions

▶ Riders must be able to start, halt, and rein their horses to play this game. Most riders learn this during their first mounted lesson.

▶ There should be adequate room for horses to line up side by side at the end of the ring, with at least one horse-length of space between each. Horses that squabble should not be next to one another.
▶ There should be enough room beyond the finish line to avoid congestion. Riders should know where to go after they cross the finish line, for example, to turn left, and line up again.
▶ Trot/jog gait should be used only when all riders can ride safely at that gait.
▶ Try to ride the Hare Race in a direction away from the barn; otherwise, horses may race to the barn.
▶ Canter/lope gait is not recommended — it simulates a stampede.

# Tips

▶ The Hare Race helps riders who have difficulty keeping their horses in motion.
▶ To reinforce learning, have riders teach each other how they use their natural aids (i.e., seat, hands, legs, feet, voice, and weight).

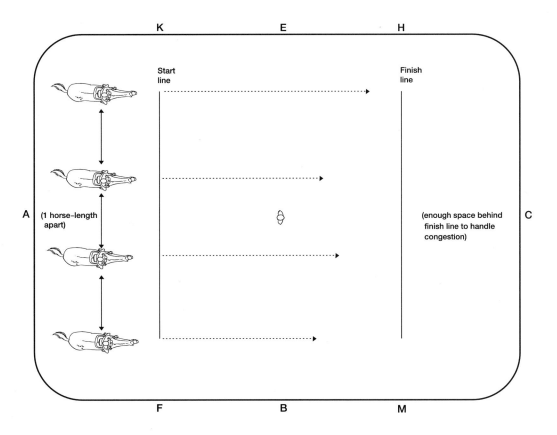

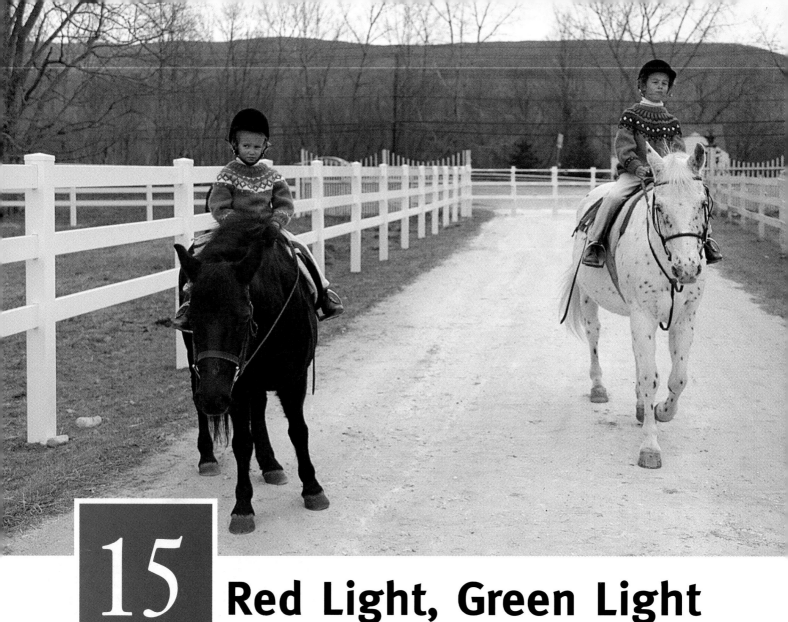

# 15

# Red Light, Green Light

▶ **B e g i n n i n g   R i d e r s**

In this popular game that many of us played as kids, the instructor (or a rider) acts as a vocal traffic light, calling out "Green light" to start the riders, then "Red light" to stop them wherever they are. The goal is to reach the finish line as quickly as possible without getting caught moving on a red light. In this horsey version, riders must be able to get their horses moving quickly and halted promptly. We tell riders that horses must keep "four on the floor" at the halt, or they'll have to go back to the start line. The winner is usually the rider to get a slight jump on the competition.

## PURPOSE

Teaches the rider to start, stop, maintain a halt, and rein in a straight line.

# Instructions

1. Instructor establishes start line at one end of ring, finish line at opposite end, and gait (walk or trot).
2. Instructor or rider stands behind finish line to act as "traffic light." A second instructor or rider stands at start line to watch and assist riders.
3. Riders line up at start line facing "traffic light."
4. "Traffic light" says, "Green light."
5. Riders move their horses at designated gait toward the finish line. Horse and rider must return to start line if horse changes to faster gait.
6. After 5–7 seconds, "traffic light" says, "Red light."
7. Riders halt within a 3-second audible count of the "red light" command. Horse and rider must return to start line if horse fails to halt or moves after halting.
8. "Traffic light" continues giving start and halt commands.
▸ **Winner:** The first rider to cross the finish line.

# Cautions

▸ Start with a walk-only race before allowing jog or trot.
▸ Lope/canter is not recommended.
▸ Adjust the halting time if needed to discourage students from quick-halting their horses (i.e., pulling too severely on a horse's mouth).
▸ In their zeal to win, even with a longer halt time, riders may try to quick-halt their horses. To prevent this, tell riders that if a horse raises his head above that of his rider, the rider will be disqualified.

# Tips

▸ Have the winner become the "traffic light" for the next game.
▸ Challenge better riders with a start-time handicap.
▸ Be sure "traffic light" uses an audible halt count (e.g., "one thousand one, one thousand two").
▸ Horses are usually allowed to move one foot without disqualification after the stop.

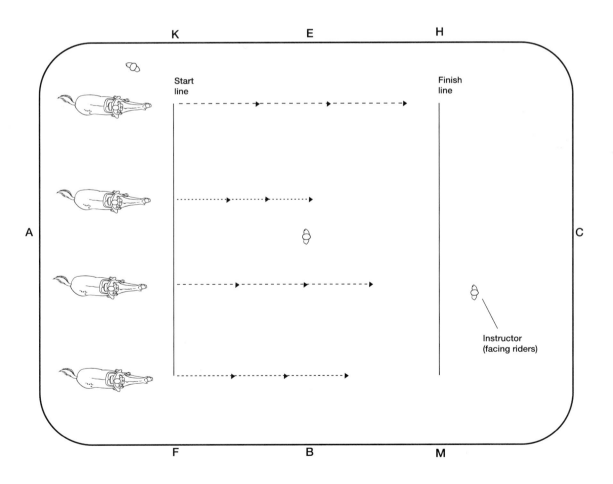

# 16 Saddle-Up Race

▶ **Beginning Riders**

Who can tack up and mount the fastest? A great game for building teamwork, cooperation, and group participation, the Saddle-Up Race can be used as a motivator when teaching this skill. A desire to win will have everyone listening carefully to riders' suggestions and tips on how to saddle up quickly and correctly, not always the most exciting topic. This is a great rainy day, limited riding area game when everyone is forced indoors.

### PURPOSE

Teaches careful, efficient saddling in a way that students are sure to remember.

# Instructions

1. Students divide into pairs; each pair teams up with a bridled horse. One student will saddle and ride the horse; the other will hold and lead the horse.
2. Instructor establishes start/finish line at one end of ring.
3. Horses are positioned at start/finish line, one horse-length apart. Saddles are placed on ground, covered by pads, at the opposite end of the ring. One team member holds horse at reins; the other team member is the "rider."
4. Riders line up on foot next to saddles.
5. Instructor announces gait for race and signals for game to begin.
6. Leaders quickly walk horses to partner and saddle.
7. Riders tack up their horses (which are held by partners), mount, and ride back to start/finish line (or designated "parking place") as quickly as possible. Improper saddling means disqualification.
   ‣ **Winner:** First rider to cross start/finish line.

# Cautions

‣ Be sure all players have had a saddling lesson prior to game. Staff must check saddling before allowing rider to mount to avoid a spill.
‣ Riders must be physically able to lift saddle onto horse's back.
‣ Use tolerant, reliable horses that are willing to be bumped while being saddled and aren't fussy about being cinched up.
‣ Be well organized; supervise carefully.
‣ Don't run behind horse when adjusting girth.
‣ Match riders to horses — small riders tack up and ride small horses. Provide assistance hoisting saddle onto horse if needed.

# Variations

‣ For limited space, have saddles on ground near horses. First team to mount a rider wins.
‣ Have the partner unsaddle the horse. The rider rides bareback to the other end of the ring and back to the saddling area, where the horse is resaddled.
‣ Mounted rider rides to partner at opposite end and unsaddles. Partner mounts bareback, rides length of ring and back; team resaddles horse and first rider mounts again.

# Tips

‣ Position saddles in area of ring closest to tack room.
‣ Place saddles on tarp to protect them from sand/grass.
‣ For Western saddles, loop girth and stirrups over saddle or hook over saddle horn while placing on horse.
‣ Use lighter weight English saddles for small riders.
‣ Always use proper lifting technique: bend knees and keep back straight.

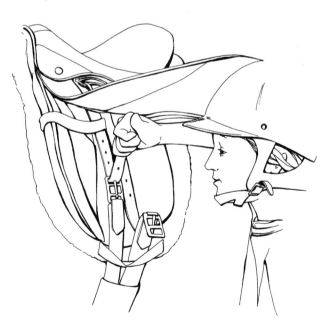

The saddle must be secured snugly and correctly before a rider mounts.

# 17 "No Hands" Contest

▶ Intermediate Riders

This is an amusing game, requiring considerable skill. It's best played by a group of four to six riders in a large ring. It shows riders that it's possible to direct a horse without using the reins, relying instead on leg, seat, and weight aids. It also gives riders an incentive to figure out what works and how to communicate with their horse.

Most riders find that by "scissoring" their legs, twisting their hips, and using weight shifts, they can direct their horses without touching the reins. Later on, they may try figure eights and other patterns.

Directing a horse without reins is a very challenging skill. This game may be played individually. At higher levels, a single rider may do Dressage Training Level Test I or reining pattern.

### PURPOSE

Improves the use of leg aids and balance, and teaches the rider to "rein" without using the reins.

# Instructions

1. Riders practice riding without reins following instructor's commands to turn, halt, start, and finally "park" in the center.
2. Instructor describes a simple pattern. For example, "Walk to the fence. Turn left. At the end, do a circle around the barrel. Walk two horse-lengths past your 'parking place,' reverse direction, and park."
3. Riders attempt pattern one at a time. Two riders may attempt pattern as long as they proceed in opposite directions.
   ▸ **Winner:** Rider completing the pattern in the least amount of time without reins.

# Caution

Beginning riders should have hands on reins at all times in case of trouble but should use reins only to avoid other riders; for example, to avoid crowding or a convergence of horses. Intermediate riders would also be wise to keep hands on reins.

# Variations

▸ Add more complex patterns. Include halt or trot from one point to another.
▸ Try pairs riding together, perhaps with a ribbon.
▸ Try Dressage Training Level Test I.
▸ Ride around cones, poles, or barrels — a visual aid helps.

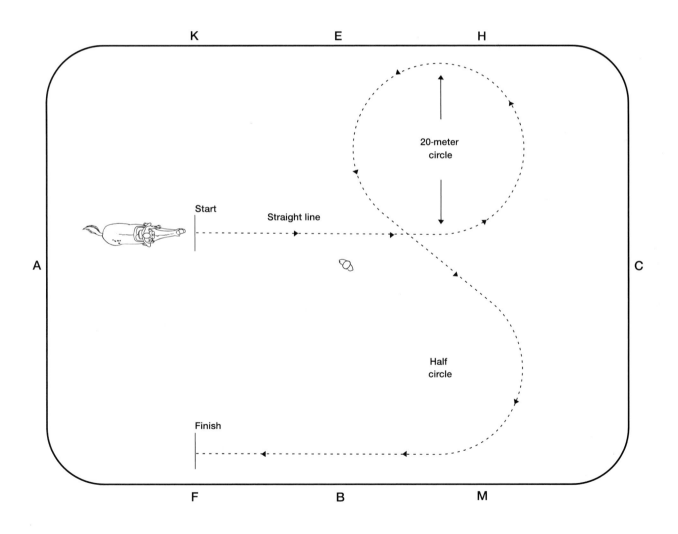

# 18 Tennis Tournament

▶ **Intermediate Riders**

Similar to Egg 'n' Spoon, this game is best played at the walk. Riders attempt to balance a tennis ball on a racquet and deposit it in a bucket at the other end of the arena. Riders with steady hands may be able to play it at the trot, but no one can canter this game!

# Instructions

1. Mounted riders line up at one end of ring, where they're given tennis racquet and tennis ball.
2. Instructor establishes finish line and places bucket at other end of ring.
3. Instructor signals for game to begin.
4. Each rider balances tennis ball on racquet while riding to finish line, then drops ball in bucket. If ball rolls off racquet, rider dismounts, retrieves ball, remounts, and places ball on racquet unaided.
 ▸ **Winner:** First rider to drop tennis ball into the bucket.

# Cautions

▸ Horses must be accustomed to racquets and to balls dropping nearby. If horses get "big eyed" or scared, they must be desensitized before playing.
▸ Allow extra space between horses.
▸ Instruct riders not to wave racquets when around horses.

# Variations

▸ Add or allow a trot.
▸ Make it an elimination game such as Egg 'n' Spoon.
▸ Have riders hold the racquet in their nondominant hand to make the game more challenging.
▸ Make it a team relay.

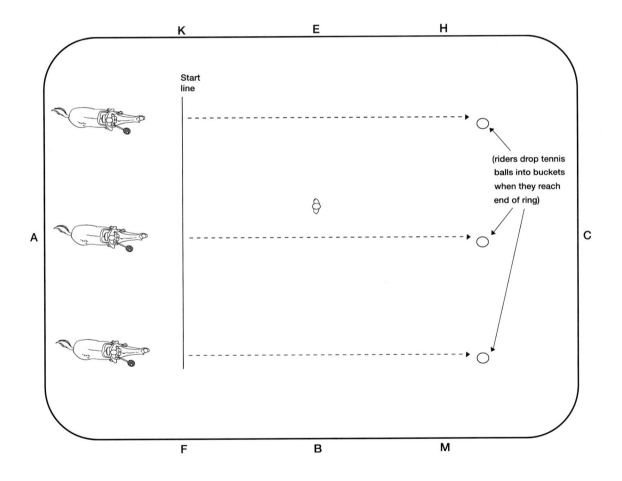

© Joyce Chartier

# Pony Cart Race

▶ **Intermediate Riders**

And they're off! This horse race requires ponies or minihorses and carts; two carts are best, but if running the race as a timed game only one cart is needed. Put two drivers in each cart to double the fun. Races are best held in a large ring. The course can be an oval lap (with cones on the corners to eliminate shortcuts) or a straight run.

# Instructions

1. Set up a course with two start/finish lines; cones work well (e.g., a cart starting at E will finish at B and vice versa).
2. Harness ponies to carts, and select a driver for each cart.
3. Position each cart on its start line.
4. Instructor announces gait for race and signals for race to begin.
5. Drivers maneuver carts along courses at appropriate gait.

▸ **Winner:** The first cart to cross its finish line.

# Cautions

▸ Driving is different from riding and requires knowledge of correct harnessing and cart handling.
▸ Drivers *must* wear helmets! Carts can tip over!

▸ *Never* canter; only walk or trot.
▸ Initially ponies should be led by instructors or assistant until drivers prove competent.
▸ Wide turns and maintaining a careful distance between the cart and fence or any obstacles are critical.
▸ Carts require smooth ground, with no ruts or holes. It is advisable to walk a course before running a cart on it.
▸ Only experienced cart drivers should race side by side.

# Variations

▸ Drivers or teams of drivers change after one lap or on the return stretch.
▸ Increase the difficulty by having drivers maneuver a course involving turns and obstacles.

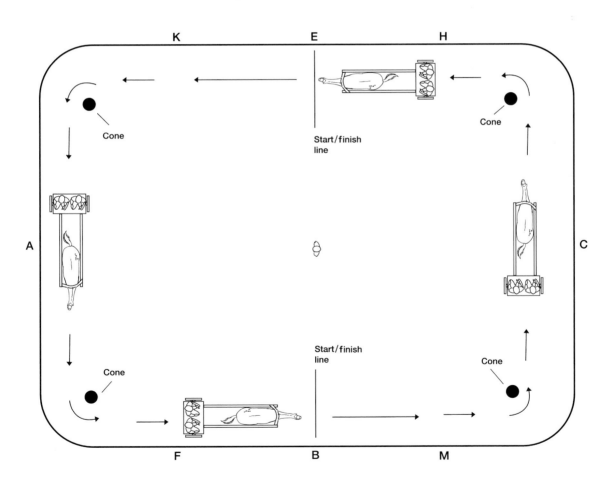

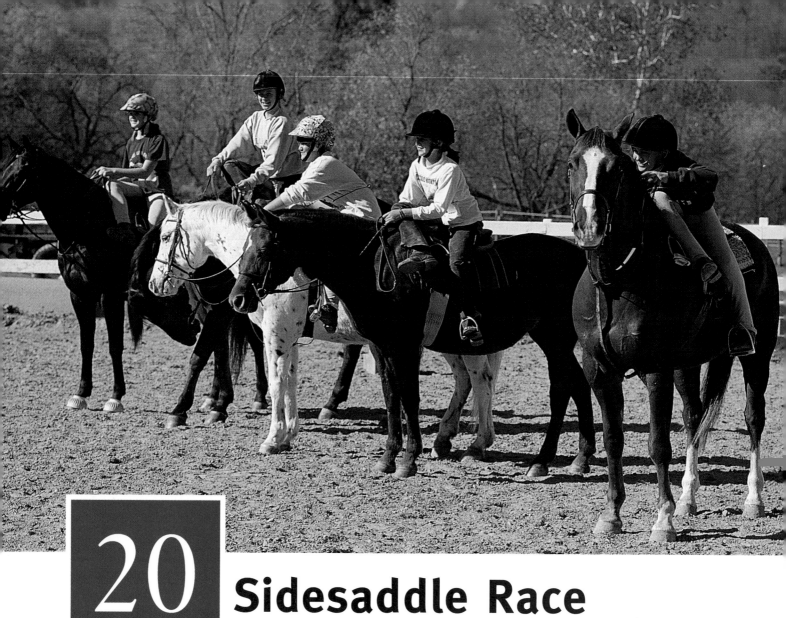

# 20 Sidesaddle Race

▶ **Advanced Riders Only**

Once riders can do Around the World, riding sidesaddle will seem relatively easy. In this race, riders get a sense of what true sidesaddle riding is like and learn how it affects balance.

Riders need to have a good, well-balanced seat and be able to start, halt, and rein easily. A relaxed rider who can move with the horse and use his or her hands and legs independently of balancing on the saddle will prevail here.

# Instructions

1. Establish start and finish lines at opposite ends of ring.
2. Riders mount their horses in sidesaddle position, with or without a saddle, and line up at start lines.
3. On the word "Go," riders ride to the finish line at a brisk walk. If riders slide off, they may remount without assistance.
   - **Winner:** First rider to reach finish line.

# Cautions

- Peacock or other safety stirrups are highly recommended for this game.
- Steady horses that are unlikely to "scoot" or move quickly are best for this event.
- Allow plenty of space between horses.
- If safety stirrups are not available, advise riders *not* to use the stirrup, as their foot might get caught. It's better to balance on the right seat bone and lean slightly right.
- This race is best done at a walk, as balance is difficult to maintain for most riders.

# Variations

- Incorporate stops, as in Red Light, Green Light.
- Ride with no stirrups.
- Have riders switch position to other side of horse.

Riders may be surprised when first sitting sidesaddle, but balance comes quickly.

Peacock or other safety stirrups should be used in this game.

# 21 Rescue Race

▶ **Advanced Riders Only**

Good guys to the rescue! Your buddy is trapped, captured, or perhaps injured, and it's up to you to get him home. In life-and-death emergencies, double riding is sometimes done. Here, you help your partner mount up and lead him back home.

This game requires good horsemanship, mounting, and dismounting skills. Buddies are tied with easily breakable ribbon (crepe-paper ribbon works well) for quick release and emergency escape.

# Instructions

1. Riders are paired into teams of two. Teams decide who will be the rescuer and who will be the captive.
2. Rescuers stand with horses at start/finish line; captives are "tied" to fence or waiting behind line from point K to F.
3. Instructor indicates gait of game (i.e., walk or jog/trot), and signals start of game.
4. Rescuers ride to K–F line, dismount, lead horses to captive, release and help captive mount the horse, and lead horse back to start/finish line.

▶ **Winner:** First team back to the start line.

# Cautions

▶ Allow plenty of room for rescuers and captives. Use four teams only in a 60- by 120-foot (18.3- by 36.6-meter) arena.
▶ Captives should be tied with easily escapable ribbon. Tie hands in front, *not* behind back.
▶ Captives can stand behind barrels or jump standards as protection from horse.
▶ Canter/lope is not recommended.
▶ Rescuers must know how to give a leg-up mount. (See page 33.)

# Variation

Run this race as a bareback event at walk or trot.

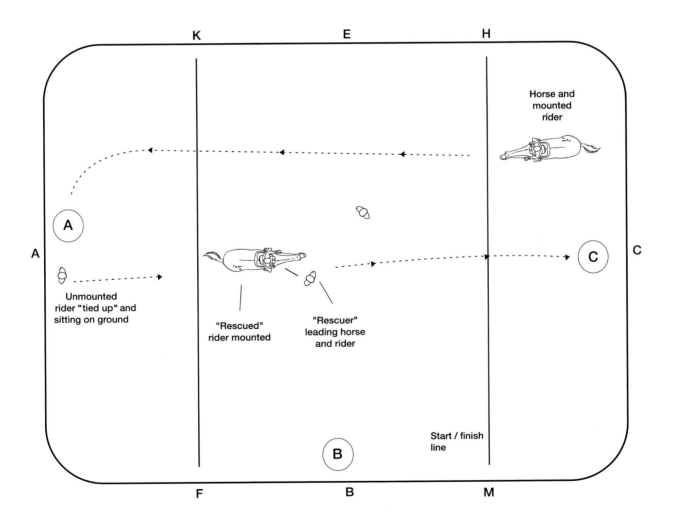

# IV

# Relay Races

Horses love to run. New foals in pasture test their gangly, unsteady legs almost immediately. Running from danger or for sheer joy is something horses do naturally. Relay races funnel that boundless energy into a structured framework that hastens the physical and psychological development of horse and rider.

Riding should be fun. Running is a part of riding that comes over time, with developing horsemanship skills. Relay races challenge and stimulate a rider's interest, teach control of the horse, and develop alertness, cooperation, and good sportsmanship. Experience the glow of achievement by winning a relay race; feel a sense of purpose in imitating the old Pony Express race by delivering the mail on time!

There are many things to consider before entering a relay race. Attitude comes first. Ask yourself if this is going to be fun. Do you understand what you are expected to do? Are you a good sport? Is winning the most important part of the race? Are you happy with your horse? Do you think he will give willing cooperation? If the horse you are to ride is not your choice but your instructor's, do you think you can teach the horse to enjoy the game with you? A positive attitude is often the key to winning a race or having a good time.

In relay races, instructors have an opportunity to teach much more than just a fun game. By being sensitive to riders' attitudes, instructors can teach riders some of life's most important skills. Teach with a smile, give clear, concise explanations, and encourage fair play and good sportsmanship. Most of all, have fun!

## Equipment Needed for Games

- Shoes, sneakers, boots
- Buckets
- Potatoes
- Tubs
- Barrels (55-gallon [250-liter] drums)
- Minnow nets
- Polocrosse rackets
- Jugs
- Plastic cups
- Root beer
- Water
- Catalogs
- Mounting block
- Mail sack (backpack, fanny pack, saddle-bag)
- "Letters" (paper or cardboard with "address")
- Crop, stick, or baton
- Cones
- Carrots, apples, alfalfa cubes, etc.
- Stick or bamboo cane
- "Trash" (cans, buckets, etc.)

◀ Veggie Stew challenges the skill of the rider and the willpower of the horse: Doesn't that carrot look tasty?

# 22 Boots in the Bucket

▶ **Beginning Riders**

Grab a shoe or boot off the fence and drop it in a bucket. Sounds simple enough, doesn't it? How good are your aim and your reining? All you need to play this game are two big buckets and some old shoes or boots (or just about anything unbreakable). If you can get your horse moving and can direct him where you want him to go, you'll excel at this game.

This is a good training exercise for beginners trying to learn neck reining. Riders need to think ahead as they rein toward the boots, ride one-handed, reach out, grab, carry, and drop the boot in the bucket. In this game, riders who typically focus only on the horse below must focus on another object, maintain balance while reaching slightly, and maneuver one-handed to a specific spot. Beginners are challenged at a slow gait, but good riders may want to step up the pace. As the speed of the game increases, so does the challenge.

### PURPOSE

Improves rider's reining ability and rider's ability to keep horse at a certain gait.

# Instructions

1. Line up old shoes or boots along the ring wall or on fence posts in various places. Place buckets at various locations, and designate each for a team.
2. Instructor establishes start/finish line(s). (The start/finish may be the same line or can be set at opposite ends of the ring.)
3. While riding at a walk around the ring, riders count off by twos, establishing two teams.
4. Instructor announces gait for game and signals riders to begin.
5. A rider from each team tries to grab a shoe or boot with outside hand (hand by the fence or rail), and then tries to drop it into the bucket designated for his or her team. (If buckets are placed inside the track, riders may have to transfer the boot to the other hand.) If shoe or boot misses bucket, rider must dismount, grab boot, remount, and make another attempt. Team scores a point for each bucketed shoe or boot.
6. Each rider returns to start/finish line and tags next teammate, who repeats the circuit; the game continues in relay fashion until all boots or shoes are in buckets.

▶ **Winner:** Team with the most points at end of relay.

# Cautions

▶ Horses must be accustomed to objects being tossed from their backs and to the sound of boots hitting the bucket.
▶ Adjust the game's gait and complexity to the ability of the riders.
▶ Advise riders to rein horses close to boots and buckets rather than stretching and risking loss of balance.
▶ Riders should not stop or circle around if they miss a boot, unless rules specify only one rider in ring at a time.

# Variations

▶ Adjust the pace — let them race! Require riders to travel at a designated gait only when grabbing shoes and making the drop.

▶ Place the bucket in a hard-to-navigate spot (for example, in a three-sided box defined by poles).
▶ Line up two teams facing point A or C, with teammates behind first rider along wall to points E and B. Each team sends one rider at a time. When boot is dropped in bucket, next team member begins.
▶ In one-at-a-time relay, require riders to dismount, pick up boot, remount, and try again if boot drops or misses bucket.
▶ Place boots on the ground rather than on a fence post. Riders dismount, grab a boot, remount, ride to bucket, and drop boot in.
▶ On trail rides, a simple prop, such as twine, grass, a pine cone, or a bandanna can be picked up and moved to a new location. The lead rider (instructor) tells the group what the object is, then places it on a tree branch or other reachable spot. Each rider in turn picks up the object and places it down the trail for the next rider to retrieve. (If object drops to ground, it is left there to avoid delaying entire group.) Beware of tree branches that might whip the next rider in line.

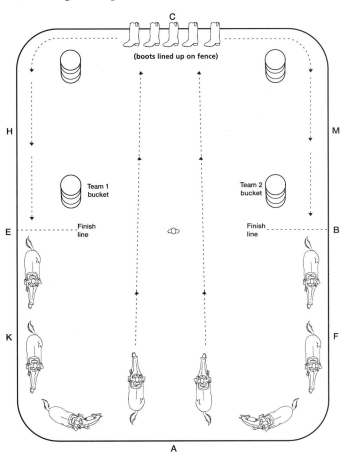

# 23 Catalog Race

▶ **Beginning Riders**

If you don't know what to do with all the catalogs that fill your mailbox, this is the perfect game for you. It can be a timed event or a relay race. Instructor assigns a page number for each rider to retrieve; then riders ride to a catalog, dismount, rip out a page, mount, and return the page to the instructor or put it in a designated spot.

**PURPOSE**

Teaches keenness, speed, mounting, dismounting, teamwork.

# Instructions

1. Riders divide into teams and line up at one end of ring. Catalogs — one for each team — are placed on the ground or on a barrel or mounting block at opposite end.
2. Instructor assigns a page number to each rider, announces gait, how paper is to be held, and signals for game to begin.
3. First rider of team rides to designated catalog, dismounts, and tears out a page of catalog.
4. Rider remounts, rides back to team, and next rider rides to catalog for a page. (If rider drops page, rider dismounts, picks up page, and remounts.)

▸ **Winner:** First team to have all members complete relay.

# Cautions

▸ Horses must not be bothered by flapping paper.

▸ Riders should take reins over horse's head while getting page from catalog.
▸ Riders must be careful not to get arm or hand tangled in reins.
▸ If an assistant is available, have assistant hold horse while rider removes page and help rider remount.
▸ All riders must be able to hold the paper in the designated manner.

# Variations

▸ Limited only by your creativity. You can designate a certain page of the catalog, or designate a particular drop point for the page, for example.
▸ Designate how rider is to carry page: under seat or in one hand.
▸ Require different gaits and paths to vary difficulty.

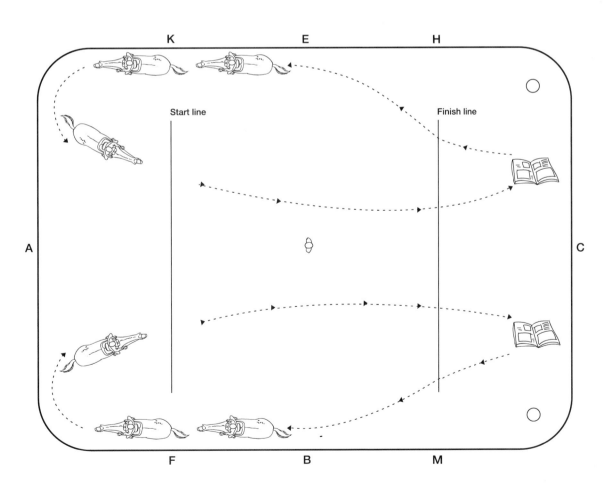

# 24

# Potato Race

▶ **Intermediate Riders**

Scoop a potato from a water-filled wash tub and take it home. A team or timed event, this game is great fun for horse and rider. Setting tubs on top of barrels makes them easier to reach. Leave tubs on the ground for a more challenging game for advanced riders only.

For a fun game with no splash, set potatoes atop upturned 55-gallon (250-liter) drums. Rider grabs potato from atop the team's drum, then takes it to the teams tub at start line and deposits it, as shown in the photgraph. First team to transfer all potatoes wins.

# Instructions

1. Riders divide into two teams.
2. Instructor places two buckets or wash tubs containing water and an equal number of potatoes in the center of the ring and one tub containing water at each end of the ring.
3. Teams, equipped with a minnow net or polocrosse racket, line up in relay fashion at opposite ends of ring next to water-filled tubs. Riders awaiting their turns are on foot, holding their horses.
4. Instructor announces gait for the race and signals for game to begin.
5. The first rider for each team mounts, rides to team's tub of potatoes, scoops up one potato, takes it to team's tub at start line, and deposits it. (If rider scoops up more than one potato, it must be returned.) Rider dismounts and hands the next teammate the net or racket; that teammate then mounts and repeats the leg.

▶ **Winner:** First team to transfer all the potatoes in tub at center of ring to tub at the start line.

# Cautions

▶ Horses must be accustomed to riders carrying sticks of any sort.
▶ Riders must be careful to avoid banging horse's head or legs with nets or rackets.
▶ Horses must be accustomed to object being tossed into water and sound of potato landing in tub and water splashing.

# Variations

▶ Riders ride to center, dismount to get potato, remount, return to start, and deposit potato.
▶ Tubs sit atop 55-gallon (250-liter) drums; riders reach for potatoes with hands rather than scooping them up with nets or rackets.
▶ Instructor announces that potato stealing is okay. Riders steal the other team's potatoes. The team with the most when time is called wins.

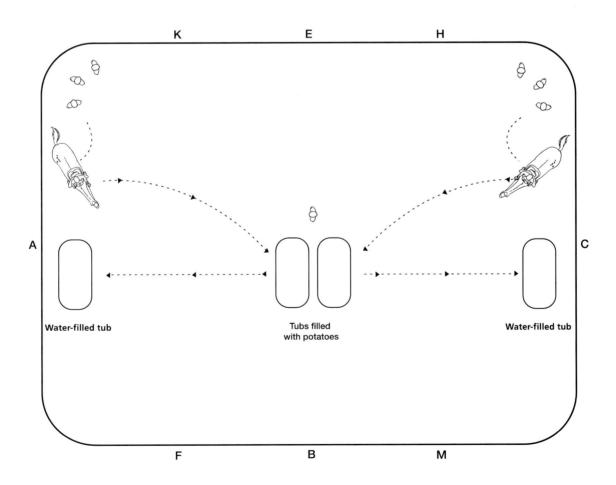

# 25 Root Beer Relay

▶ **Intermediate Riders**

Root Beer Relay can be either a team or a timed event with two or more riders. Riders try to fill a jug with root beer, one cup at a time. (Make sure the jug is clean!) The team with the most root beer wins. Winners get to drink all the root beer!

> **PURPOSE**
>
> Promotes skillful riding, quiet seat and hands, and good balance.

# Instructions

1. Instructor divides riders into equal teams.
2. Teams line up in relay fashion at one end of ring; their designated jugs are placed at the other end. Each team is equipped with 1 quart (.95 liter) of root beer and one plastic cup.
3. Instructor announces gait for race and signals for game to begin.
4. First rider mounts, is handed a cup filled with root beer, rides to the other end of the ring, and pours root beer into his or her team's jug.
5. Rider rides back to teammates, dismounts, fills cup with root beer, and hands cup to next mounted teammate. Game continues until all riders on each team have finished their leg of relay.
   ▸ **Winner:** Team whose jug holds the most root beer.

# Cautions

▸ Horses must not be bothered by getting wet.
▸ This game can get goofy and silly: Control the participants by stating rules clearly and setting limits.
▸ If concerned about getting saddle wet, use water instead of root beer or ride bareback.

# Variations

▸ The game is timed, and riders continue relay until time is up.
▸ Difficulty of the game varies with the size and fullness of the cups and the size of the jug opening. Start with a wide-mouthed jug, then use jugs with narrower openings to add more difficulty.
▸ The jug is placed on a barrel, held by someone, or hangs from a string or fishing pole.
▸ Riders ride faster or through a pattern, or they mount and dismount with cup in hand.
▸ Substitute water for root beer, and make this a bareback event. Horses enjoy this on a hot summer's day.
▸ Empty cups held by teammates are substituted for empty jugs. Teammates start at opposite ends of ring; both are on horseback. First rider rides with full cup of water to teammate, pours water into teammate's empty cup, and rides back to other end of ring. Teammate repeats pattern. They make four or five trips back and forth; team with fullest cup of water at the end wins.

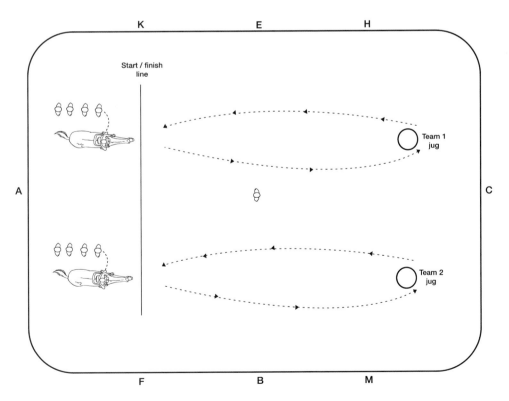

# Pony Express Relay

▶ **Intermediate Riders**

It is 1860. You have just been hired as a rider for the Pony Express, a rapid postal delivery system in the western United States. Imagine what your days will be like — your sense of duty and adventure, the problems you might encounter along the way. Will rain, sleet, or snow keep you from your appointed rounds?

Pony Express Relay is an adaptation of the old-time Pony Express. Each Pony Express team "delivers" the contents of a mail sack, backpack, fanny pack, or saddlebag to people in the ring or to specific locations around the barn.

**PURPOSE**

Teaches riders to maneuver independently of others and to move off in different directions, in order to take the shortest route and arrive at a destination in the least amount of time.

# Instructions

1. Prepare "letters": pieces of paper or cardboard with an "address" written on each. Addresses can be specific people or locations in ring.
2. Riders divide into two teams and mount, standing near each other. Instructor supervises.
3. "Mail sacks" are stuffed with an equal number of letters and distributed to each team.
4. Instructor announces gait and signals for game to begin.
5. First rider holds sack, pulls out a letter, delivers it, and returns to team. Rider must carry sack to destination; if it is dropped, rider must dismount, pick it up, and remount.
6. Rider passes sack to teammate, who repeats delivery process. Pony Express continues until all letters are delivered.
   ▸ **Winner:** First team to deliver all the mail.

# Cautions

▸ Tailor game's speed and complexity to riders' ability.
▸ Be sure horses won't spook if "letter" or mail sack is dropped.
▸ If mail sack is fastened to saddle, be sure it won't hinder rider's ability to maneuver or dismount.

# Tips

▸ Be sure that all the papers in the sack are deliverable.
▸ With Western saddle, mail sack should be held on horn. With English saddle, mail sack should be attached to D-ring on off side or carried in one hand.

# Variations

▸ Play over a large expanse of land and fields, with other riders positioned to relay the mail to the next location. Three or four locations may take 1 hour or more for the game. Locations for mail transfer may be ½ mile (806.5 meters) or more apart.
▸ Set up real mailboxes on a course.

Delivering multiple pieces of mail to the same "address" is especially challenging. Be careful not to drop anything!

# 27 Stick Relay

**▶ Intermediate Riders**

As in relay events in track and field, in the Stick Relay riders work together with their teammates to complete the relay first. In this game, teams of four to six riders play the relay with a crop (24–30 inches [61–76 centimeters] long is best), baton stick, or other straight and easily retrieved object. A large wooden spoon works well.

# Instructions

1. Riders line up head-to-tail in two rows about 20 feet (6.1 m) apart, facing the instructor who stands at the opposite end holding two sticks.
2. Instructor announces gait and signals for game to begin.
3. First rider in each row rides to the instructor, receives stick, circles ring to left or right (avoiding collision with other rider), returns stick to instructor, and returns to lineup.
4. Relay race continues until all members of each team have carried stick around ring and returned to lineup.

   ▶ **Winner:** Team completing relay first.

# Cautions

▶ For safety, caution riders to slow to walk as each approaches instructor, or set cones 20 to 30 feet before instructor to indicate "walk."

▶ Riders must maintain safe distance from other riders throughout game.

▶ Don't allow riders to carry crop or baton in teeth.

# Tips

▶ Use leather-covered crops to protect hands of riders and instructors.

▶ When rider takes stick, baton, or crop from instructor, he or she must circle to the outside (left or right) to avoid running into opponent. Riders turning wrong direction must return to instructor, then turn correctly.

▶ Place buckets or cones at the corners of the ring to discourage riders from cutting corners when their excitement runs high. Riders will be disqualified for cutting corners.

# Variations

▶ Place two barrels on course (see diagram) for a rider-to-rider team relay. Riders from each team proceed around barrel, circle the ring one time, pass the stick to the next rider, then return to parking spot, facing opposite direction.

▶ Place poles or cones on course to add variety or slow the pace in one or both directions.

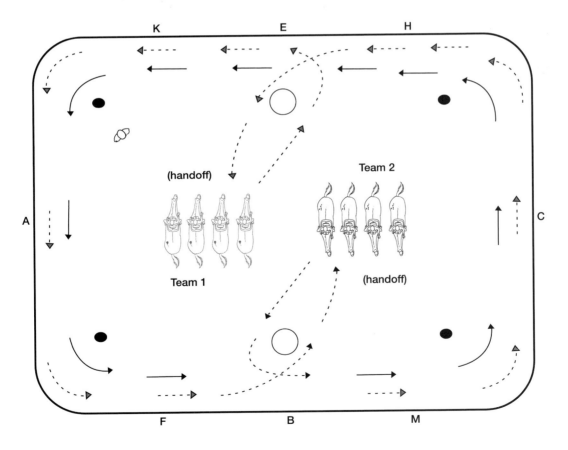

# 28 Veggie Stew

▶ **Intermediate Riders**

Cooking has never been this exciting! Similar to the Potato Race, in Veggie Stew riders are given a shopping bag and take turns going to the "store" to get ingredients for a special "stew" for horses. Select large carrots, apples, alfalfa cubes, small bags of grain or sweet feed. (Avoid sugar cubes and candy.) Perhaps the greatest challenge of this game is keeping horses from eating "stew" before dinner time. Reward horses with a bit of stew when they are untacked. Bon appétit!

**PURPOSE**

Improves coordination, balance, dexterity; encourages teamwork.

# Instructions

1. A variety of "ingredients" is placed on two barrels in the ring, one for each team. Another upturned barrel, the "stew kettle," is placed at the opposite end of ring, one for each team.
2. Riders count off to establish teams. Even-numbered riders form one team; odd-numbered riders form the other team. Teams are situated at least 20 feet (6.1 meters) apart at start/finish line.
3. First rider rides to ingredients, picks up one, puts it into sack, rides to stew kettle, removes ingredient from sack, and places it on top of stew kettle. A rider who fumbles an ingredient must dismount, pick up ingredient, and return to start/finish line to begin again. After three unsuccessful tries, rider is disqualified.
4. Rider returns to start/finish line and passes bag to next rider.
   ▶ **Winner:** Team to finish relay first.

# Cautions

Excessive noise may startle horses. Be sure that all horses are sensitized to sound of ingredients being placed onto "stew kettle" and to dropped objects.

# Variations

▶ Play game as a timed event. See which team can make the fastest stew. The first team to deposit all of its ingredients on top of the stew kettle wins.
▶ Instructor designates specific ingredients for stew. Winner is team that whips up the fastest stew.

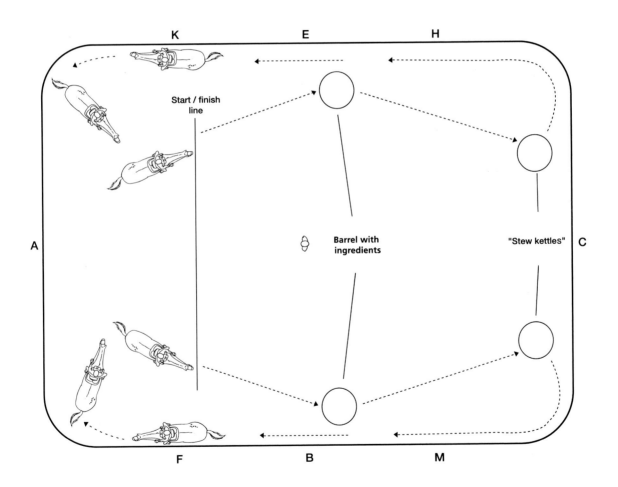

# 29 Litter Control Campaign

▶ Advanced Riders Only

A sometimes frustrating, always challenging game, Litter Control Campaign encourages riders to keep the stable area tidy and clear of debris. Once riders get the knack, this game can be played on the trail, to help keep our open spaces clean and beautiful.

### PURPOSE

Challenges riders' ability to rein, hold horse steady, and maintain balance; good training for polo events.

# Instructions

1. Scatter litter in the form of tin cans, boxes, or plastic bags in center of ring. Place a trash container for each team at equal distances from ring's center.
2. First rider from each team starts at team's container; teammates remain outside the ring. Each rider is equipped with a blunt-ended 3- to 4-foot (.9- to 1.2-meter) long stick, bamboo cane, polocrosse racket, or minnow net to scoop up trash.
3. Instructor announces gait and signals for game to begin.
4. Riders ride to center, pick up a piece of litter on end of stick, ride back to container, and dispose of it. Riders must remain mounted and must not touch litter with hand at any time. If container is knocked over, rider must dismount, right the container, and put all litter back into it by hand.
5. After depositing trash, rider rides to teammate next in line, hands off stick (or other implement), and relay continues.
6. Riders continue to clean up until all litter is collected or until time is called.
▶ **Winner:** Team that collects most trash.

# Cautions

▶ Ensure that horses are accustomed to the sounds of "noisy" litter, particularly plastic and metal, and to riders wielding sticks.
▶ If picking up litter outside of ring, riders must be aware of other potential hazards, such as dogs, cars, and so on.

# Variations

▶ Use your imagination! Virtually anything will do. Add obstacles to ring for a more challenging game.
▶ Have riders police area around stable.

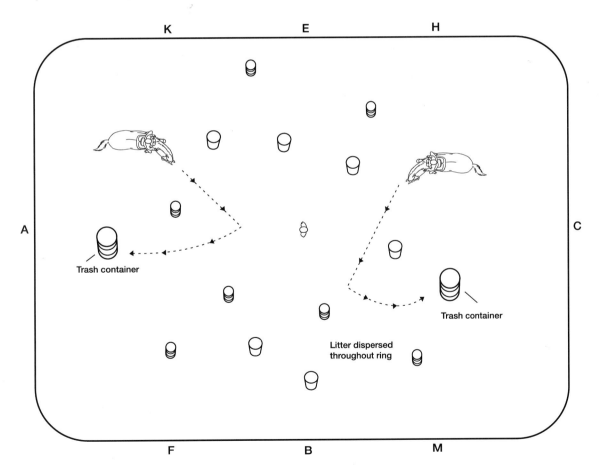

# V

# Timed Games

At our family ranch and riding school in Wisconsin, time is very important. All activities — riding, training, campouts, horse shows, and competitive distance rides — involve some component of time.

Timed games are ruled by the clock. As such, to participate in timed events, riders must be ready mentally, prepared physically, and calm yet eager emotionally.

In the heat of a race, whether you are the sole contestant or have a partner or team, remember that speed is essential but not necessary to win. The winner may well be determined by the accuracy of his or her ride. If you miss a pole, or take the wrong turn around a barrel, or the flag you stuck in the sand bucket falls out, you will be eliminated. Learn from your mistakes — they are our greatest teachers.

When riding in timed events, be especially considerate of your horse. How does he feel today? Does he exhibit your same level of enthusiasm? Is he chomping at the bit to get going? Give him a rub on the neck, a stroke of encouragement, and speak to him in a gentle voice if he is too excited. On the other hand, if he is raring — or worse yet, rearing — to go, take him for a quiet walk or consider riding a different horse. Camps and stables usually have many horses available. If the unruly mount belongs to you, do some more training before entering speed events. Enter only the events for which your coach or instructor feels you are ready.

Speed-event horses familiar with a particular event should *not* be used for beginning riders. (See specific game cautions for details.) If in doubt, an instructor should try the horse to gauge his level of action and reaction. Horse falls are a serious hazard in speed events, but proper technique greatly lessens the risk. (See specific games for details.)

## Equipment Needed for Games

- Stopwatch
- Barrels (55-gallon [250-liter] drums)
- Buckets filled with sand
- Truck and horse trailer
- Small flags
- Poles
- Jump standards
- Canvas or plastic ditch
- Oxer
- Cavalletti
- Large raincoat
- Lime or baseball-diamond chalk
- Cows
- Corral

◀ Timed games are a super way to improve needed skills. For example, skills reinforced in the Trailer Race might inspire riders to a career in search-and-rescue.

# 30 Flag Race
▶ **B e g i n n i n g   R i d e r s**

A team or timed event, in Flag Race riders attempt to move the flag from one bucket to the other. Once riders become comfortable with the speed of this fast-paced game, the instructor may choose to introduce a pattern, such as a cloverleaf, to increase difficulty.

Riders new to Flag Race might want to do a trial run using "imaginary" flags. Once this seems comfortable, try playing with the flag unfurled. Basketball players might be particularly good at this game.

## PURPOSE

Improves reining, agility, hand-eye coordination, and balance.

## Instructions

1. Place one 55-gallon (250-liter) barrel at start line and one at finish line of course. Set a bucket half-filled with sand on top of each barrel. Put a stick with a flag on one end in bucket at start line.
2. Rider lines up at start line.
3. Instructor announces gait for race and signals rider to start.
4. From the start line, rider rides to barrel, takes flag from bucket, rides prescribed course, and puts flag in opposite bucket.

▸ **Winner:** Rider with fastest time at designated gait.

## Tips

▸ The stick of the flag should be smooth or well sanded to avoid splinters. The flag is best affixed with glue to avoid possible injury.
▸ The thick end of a broom handle, cut down to about 1 foot (30 centimeters) in length, with a flag attached, makes a good flag for grabbing.

## Cautions

▸ For safety, allow only one rider on course at a time.
▸ Horses must be accustomed to flag-carrying riders. If a horse shows signs of anxiety, stop the horse and have rider either hand off or drop the flag.
▸ Beginning riders should be led until they understand the pattern and know how to grasp flag. It is usually safer to leave flag unfurled for beginning riders.

## Variations

▸ Vary the course or gait. For example, place one barrel at H and one at M. Start both teams at A. Instructor establishes course route. Be sure riders circle barrels in same direction for safety.
▸ To play with teams, set up two barrels at opposite ends of ring. Place a bucket atop each barrel, and a flag in each bucket. Teams start at opposite ends of ring, and riders put their flag in the other team's bucket when they finish the course. Team with fastest overall time wins.

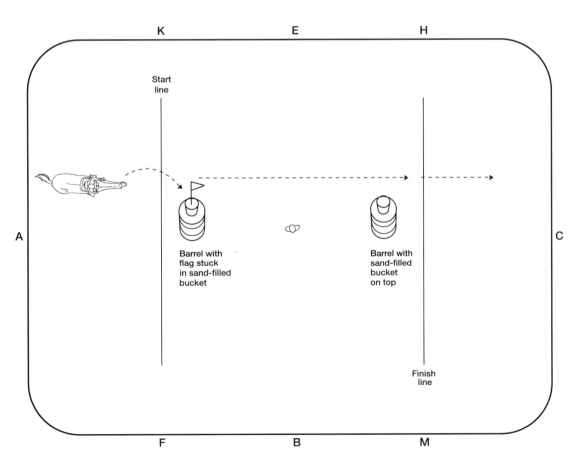

# 31 Barrel Race

▶ **Beginning Riders**

A classic speed event, this race is useful in learning how to "work" cattle into a pen and in training a horse how to maneuver around an object. This timed race can also be a team event. Three barrels are needed for each course setup. Riders proceed at a gait designated by the instructor.

An exciting rodeo event, the Barrel Race is usually done at the gallop, but beginning riders learn best at the walk or trot. Though a traditional Western event, English riders can also enjoy barrel racing, as shown above.

# Instructions

1. Instructor sets up barrels in a triangle — barrels **1** and **2** are 60 feet (18.3 meters) apart and 30 feet (9.2 meters) from the start/finish line. Barrel **3** is 120 feet (36.6 meters) from barrels **1** and **2**.
2. Riders line up within ring behind start/finish line. Gate of ring must be closed.
3. Instructor announces gait for the race and signals first rider to begin. Time starts when rider crosses start/finish line.
4. Rider proceeds from start/finish line to barrel **1**, circling it completely, then rides to barrel **2**, circling it completely in the opposite direction. The rider circles barrel **3** and returns to start/finish line.

▸ **Winner:** Rider with fastest time.

# Cautions

▸ Some school horses are former speed-event horses, trained to gallop when faced with this pattern. Such horses should be excused from this event if control is a concern. Only very skilled riders (and horses) should be allowed to run this course at full speed.

▸ Horse falls are a hazard. Reduce speed or make a wide turn when rounding barrel to minimize the possibility of such a fall.
▸ If this is a speed event, footing should be ideal for high speed, specifically fairly deep sand that can be raked up around barrels prior to next rider if deep track is a hazard.

# Variations

▸ Allowing sufficient room, set up barrel patterns for two teams and run the course as a relay race. Set one barrel near far end of the ring for each team, and establish start/finish line at opposite end of ring. Team members ride around barrel (one or more circles) and return to start line. Next teammate then rides the same pattern.
▸ Line up three barrels at start/finish line and two at the far end of the ring, and run a team or relay race. A rider from each team lines up behind the start/finish line. At the signal, riders begin. The rider on left circles center barrel first then the one on the far left, while the rider on the right circles the right barrel, then the center barrel. Both riders then race to circle their respective barrel at the far end, returning to the start/finish line. Fastest team wins.

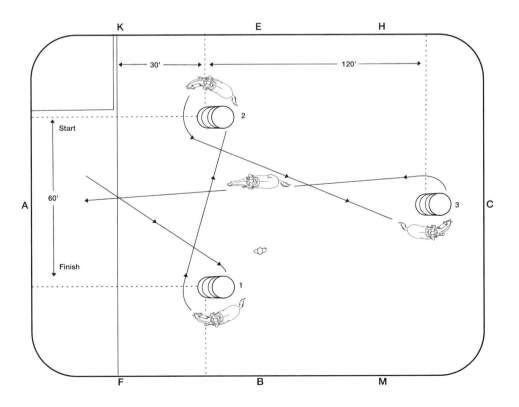

# 32 Pole Bending

▶ Beginning Riders

Another favorite timed speed event, Pole Bending requires six poles (often *jump standards*, the uprights that support jumps) or barrels. Poles anchored in a cement-filled can or poles designed specifically for this purpose are best. For beginning riders, cones work just as well.

A true test of reining and horse/rider communication, Pole Bending demands the same skill and finesse needed by downhill slalom ski racers. The goal is to ride as straight a line as possible, weaving around the poles or barrels. Poles can be arranged in a straight line or offset slightly for more of a challenge. Traditionally a timed event, you can set up two lines of poles and run a side-by-side race or run a race with teams.

> ### PURPOSE
>
> Improves reining ability, coordination of aids, sense of timing, horse/rider communication.

# Instructions

1. Instructor sets up six poles, barrels, or jump standards. Poles are set in a straight line; first pole is 20 feet (6.1 meters) from start/finish line, subsequent poles are 18 feet (5.5 meters) apart.
2. Instructor announces gait for race and signals rider to begin.
3. Rider rides length of ring around last pole and weaves left and right through poles to start/finish line, then circles first pole and weaves right and left back through poles. After rounding the last pole, rider heads straight back to start/finish line.
▸ **Winner:** Rider with fastest time.

# Cautions

▸ Trotting is best and safest. Beginning riders may walk/trot.
▸ As in barrel racing, speed-event horses should not be used with beginning riders. (See Cautions, p. 77.)

# Variations

▸ Simplify or shorten race by eliminating straight run or one weaving run.
▸ For a relay race, two lines of poles can be set up.
▸ To control speed and difficulty, poles can be placed closer together.
▸ Set up an odd number of poles. Position two teams at opposite ends of ring. Start first riders at the same time from the same side of the poles; for example, riders first weave to their right — because of the odd number of poles, riders will pass on opposite sides. Riders continue to the other end. The next team rider begins when teammate reaches the far end. First team to have all its members at the other end wins!
▸ Use fewer barrels, and require riders to do a complete circle around each barrel.

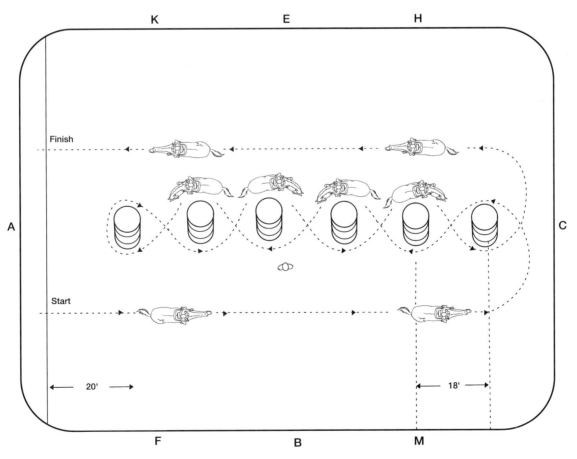

# 33 Obstacle Course

▶ Intermediate Riders

A simpler, safer version of the famous steeplechase obstacle course makes use of the natural objects and obstacles found in a field or woods as well as man-made ones in a riding arena. Simple items should be included for horses to maneuver around. A few "step-overs," but none that a horse would be inclined to jump, add challenge and interest. Riders can initially follow the leader through a course to help a reluctant horse overcome any anxiety about strange objects. Start slow and simple, and gradually add speed and complexity as horses and riders become proficient in the course.

# Instructions

1. Instructor sets up obstacles throughout ring.
2. Instructor explains in which order riders are to tackle obstacles and sets gait for race.
3. Instructor signals rider to begin, starting the timer as rider crosses start line.
4. Rider completes course as instructed; time stops as rider crosses finish line.
▸ **Winner:** Rider to complete course with fastest time.

# Tip

Rider must plan in advance and should be allowed to walk the course on foot. Accuracy and speed within safety parameters require careful visualization.

# Cautions

▸ The course should be designed for the ability of all riders in the group. Make sure riders take obstacles in the order they were designed to be ridden.
▸ Obstacles can be eliminated for beginning riders or you can request that riders proceed at a slow gait.
▸ Watch rider speed. Instruct riders to slow down if necessary.

# Variations

▸ Order of course may be changed by removing flags, or riders may choose four of eight obstacles, with instructor's approval.
▸ Good follow-the-leader event.

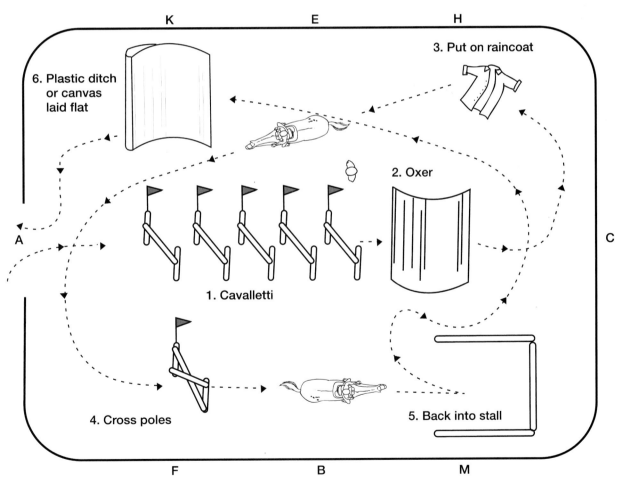

This course setup is appropriate for advanced riders only.

# 34 Flag and Sand

▶ Intermediate Riders

Combine the Barrel Race with Flag Race, and you have a dizzy version of both! In Flag and Sand, riders grab and plant the flag while circling barrels the prescribed number of times. Steering the right course and good timing are key to getting and delivering the flag.

# Instructions

1. Set up two barrels in ring, 50 to 60 feet (15.3 to 18.3 meters) apart; place bucket of sand on each. Put a stick with a flag on one end in one bucket.
2. Riders line up at opposite end of arena, behind start/finish line.
3. Instructor designates gait and number of turns around barrel, signals for game to begin, and starts timer when rider crosses start/finish line.
4. Rider rides to barrel and grabs flag while riding around barrel designated number of times, then rides to second barrel and plants flag in sand while riding around second barrel designated number of times. If flag falls out of bucket of sand, rider is eliminated.
5. Rider returns to start/finish line, and instructor stops timer.
   - **Winner:** Rider with fastest time.

# Cautions

- Some school horses are former speed-event horses, trained to gallop when faced with this pattern. Such horses should be excused from this event if control is a concern. Only very skilled riders (and horses) should be allowed to run this course at full speed.
- Horse falls are a hazard. Reduce speed or make a wide turn when rounding barrel to minimize the possibility of such a fall.
- If this is a speed event, footing should be ideal: fairly deep sand that can be raked up around barrels prior to next rider if deep track is a hazard.

# Variations

- Require riders to circle the second barrel in the opposite direction when planting the flag (requires transferring flag to the other hand, also).
- Make this a two-team event with a flag in each bucket. A rider from each team grabs a flag and takes it to the other bucket.

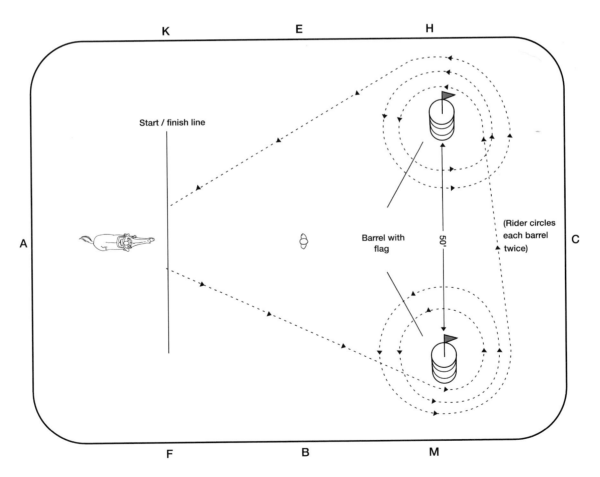

# 35

# Keyhole Race
▶ Advanced Riders Only

A challenging task for horse and rider, the Keyhole Race requires precision and speed, tempered with patience. With room for only a small margin of error, horses easily step out of "keyhole" when rider is too eager.

This race requires use of all rider aids to negotiate in and out of a tight spot. Reining, halting, and turning are particularly important.

**PURPOSE**

Improves precision and control of speed; helps impatient riders develop patience.

# Instructions

1. A 4-foot (1.2-meter) wide slot, or "keyhole," is drawn with lime or baseball-diamond chalk on ground in ring. Judge stands near keyhole. Start/finish line is designated at end of ring opposite keyhole.
2. Instructor signals rider to begin and starts timer when rider crosses start/finish line.
3. Rider moves into keyhole, turns horse 180 degrees, and rides back to the start/finish line. Rider is disqualified if horse steps on or over the edges of keyhole.

▶ **Winner:** Rider with fastest time.

# Cautions

▶ Some school horses are former speed-event horses, trained to gallop when faced with this pattern. Such horses should be excused from this event if control is a concern.
▶ Advise riders to avoid reining horse back too severely in keyhole and at finish line to avoid rearing.
▶ Eliminate fault line if it causes riders to stop too quickly.

# Variations

▶ Enlarge keyhole for beginning riders. Gradually reduce size as riders become proficient.
▶ Set up two keyholes and run as a side-by-side race. Winner is first to cross start/finish line.

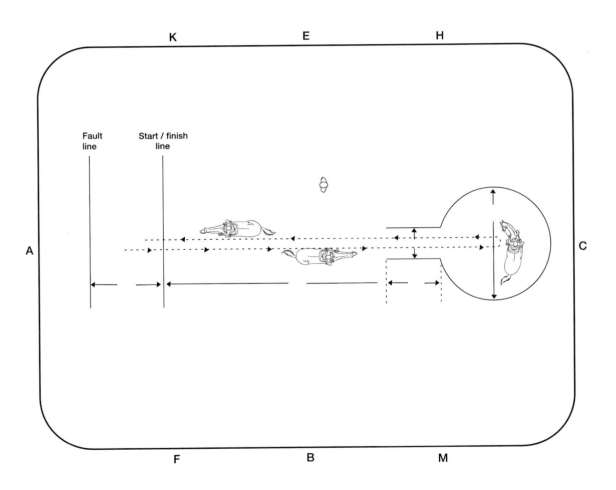

# 36 Team Penning

▶ Advanced Riders Only

Team penning simulates the ranch chores that cowboys do to sort cattle for branding, weaning, or shipping. A good horse with cow sense that will work cattle slowly is best for this nationally recognized sport. Most pennings use yearling heifers. The cattle are divided into herds of 30 or sometimes fewer. After ten runs, the cattle are removed and a fresh herd is brought in. Rules are designed to protect the cattle from harm. Line judges eliminate any rider guilty of rough play. The ring must be large enough for horses and cattle to run without slamming into fences, yet small enough so that cattle do not tire quickly.

The herd is generally bunched at the end of the ring. Cowboys ride quietly among them to condition them to the horses. When the action starts, three riders constituting a team lope down the ring as the line judge shouts the number of the heifers to be penned. Judge may shout "Five! Five! Five!", indicating that the three cattle wearing that number are to be herded into a pen at the opposite end of the ring. Riders must anticipate how the cattle will move and how to best separate their chosen heifer from the herd.

## PURPOSE

Excellent practice sorting cattle for penning — veterinary inspection, inoculation, branding.

# Instructions*

1. Set up 16- by 24-foot (4.9- by 7.3 meter) corral with a 5- to 10-foot (1.5- to 3.1-meter) opening at one end of ring.
2. Mark each heifer in a herd of 12 with numbers 1 through 4. Three heifers should be marked "1," three marked "2," and so forth until all are marked.
3. Herd is let into ring. Mounted team enters ring.
4. Instructor calls the number of the heifers to be moved into corral. (For example, if judge calls "One!," the three heifers marked "1" will be moved into corral.) Judge starts timer.
5. Team has 90 seconds to move specified heifers into corral. If they finish before time is up, they raise their hands and judge stops timer.
   - **Winner:** Team that corrals three heifers in shortest time.

# Cautions

- ▶ This game is for experienced, advanced-level riders only.
- ▶ Horses must be accustomed to cows.
- ▶ Be aware that abrupt stops and turns are common in this event.
- ▶ Avoid bumping or pushing cattle, as it may irritate cattle or horse.
- ▶ Use de-horned cattle, as an aggressive cow may challenge horse/rider.

# Variation

Rather than cattle, goats, sheep, or young horses may be used.

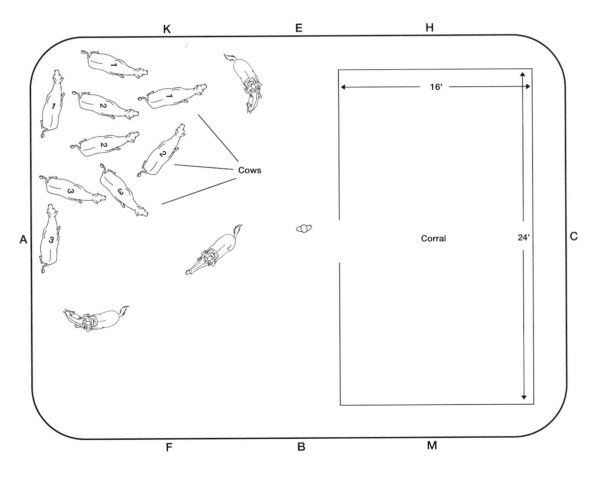

*  *Note:* These instructions and the corral size can be adjusted to suit available facility.

# 37 Trailer Race

► **Advanced Riders Only**

Need more challenge than the Saddle-up Race? How quickly can you tack-up a horse? If you can load and unload your horse from a trailer, you'll enjoy this fun race. A game no doubt invented by bored cowboys to make the day more fun, the Trailer Race is actually good training for emergency situations such as search-and-rescue where every second counts. In this timed event, riders jump from the truck cab, unload, tack, ride, untack, and reload their horse.

# Instructions

1. A truck and horse trailer are parked in the ring. Teams of two riders and one untacked horse, and tack, are also in the ring.
2. Volunteering, assignment, or drawing numbers establishes order of competitors.
3. To set up for race, first team loads untacked horse (wearing halter and lead rope) into trailer and closes trailer door.
4. Riders get into truck and close the doors.
5. Clock starts when instructor gives signal and riders open truck doors to begin the race.
6. Riders exit truck, unload horse from trailer, saddle and bridle horse. Instructor must approve proper tacking of horse before rider mounts.
7. One rider mounts and rides horse around ring (or prescribed course at prescribed gait) and back to trailer.
8. Rider dismounts and team untacks and reloads horse into trailer and closes the door.
9. Team jumps back into truck. Time stops when both doors are closed.
   ► **Winner:** Team with fastest time.

# Cautions

► Riders and horse must be experienced in loading and unloading into trailers.
► Instructor must closely supervise and coach participants.
► Riders must move carefully to avoid upsetting horse, especially when reloading horse at the end of race.
► Some cowboys load saddled horses into their trailers; this is not recommended.

# Variations

► Get several trailers and have teams compete in a head-to-head race, loading several horses.
► Instead of two riders per horse, have one rider per horse.
► Organize teams of two riders and two horses, loading both horses together in a two-horse trailer.

## RODEO STYLE

The Trailer Race can sometimes be seen at rodeos. Head-to-head competition makes the rodeo version particularly exciting — and dangerous. After racing around ring, horses' adrenaline is running. Participants must load mounts with confidence and skill to avoid rearing or refusals.

# VI

# Jumping Games

Colts in pasture will often hop over logs or branches just for the fun of it, yet carrying a rider over an obstacle is against the natural inclination of the horse. As such, after the horse is physically mature enough to start jumping with a rider, he needs careful training. Horses can be trained over cavalletti, in a jumping lane, and longed over low fences at an early age without a rider, however.

The aspiring rider who envisions leaping gracefully over a 3-foot (.9-meter) fence also needs careful training and schooling. Before jumping, horse and rider should be exposed to plenty of flat work, which we call Dressage. *Dressage*, from the French "dresser" meaning to train or drill, will teach horse and rider how to perform movements of exact dimension, such as a 10-meter (32.8-foot) circle, a near-perfect figure eight, and turns on the forehand and haunches. Dressage also teaches horse and rider how to make half-halts, accurate transitions, and improve bending. All of these skills are needed for games that require sudden turns and changes of direction.

Rhythm and tempo are important, especially in games and in jumping competition. The horse must make the corrrect approach to the fence or he will refuse, or be unwilling to take it. It is the rider's responsibility to prepare the horse to meet the obstacle in good rhythm and pacing and to arrive at the correct distance for takeoff. In the games that follow, the fences will be low to allow intermediate riders to experience the fun of jumping. Gambler's Choice and Maze Jump both challenge the rider to think, to visualize, and to plan well ahead of entering the course.

Study the course carefully. Walk the course. Plan your approach by walking on foot the sequence of jumps you wish to take. Review your plan with an instructor to ensure that you take the safest course.

As for all activities on horseback, SEI-approved headgear is vital. Many riders have been unceremoniously dumped over a fence when the horse refused. Be sure to let go of the reins if a fall is imminent — you don't want to pull the horse down with you. Also, try to tuck and roll in the case of a fall; outstretched arms can do little to help you when falling from such a height.

| Equipment Needed for Games | |
| --- | --- |
| • Barrels (55-gallon [250-liter] drums) | • Rails |
| | • Red flags |
| • Cavalletti | • Poles |
| • Jump standards | • Oxer |

◀ Jumping games are meant for advanced riders only, but spectators and riders at all levels enjoy watching these events.

# 38 Gambler's Choice

▶ **A d v a n c e d  R i d e r s  O n l y**

This game isn't called Gambler's Choice for nothing! Riders compete for the highest score, earning points for completing jumps successfully and being penalized for knockdowns, taking jumps twice or in the wrong direction, refusals, and exceeding the time limit. Because the more difficult jumps earn more points, you will find the contestants carefully planning their course and calculating the number of points they think they can earn.

# Instructions

1. Set up ten jumps in ring, each with a red flag on its right to indicate direction in which jump is to be executed. (Jumps are to be taken with red flag on rider's right.) Establish a start/finish line.
2. Riders assemble behind start/finish line.
3. Instructor signals first rider to begin, starting timer as rider crosses start/finish line.
4. Rider attempts as many jumps as possible, without jumping any twice. Jumps do not have to be taken in a specific order, but they must be taken in the correct direction (flag on right).
5. Instructor announces when there are 5 seconds left.
6. Rider returns to start/finish line. Overtime penalty is 5 points for every second over allotted time.
 ▸ **Winner:** Rider with greatest number of points.

# Scoring

 ▸ A single rail at 1 foot (.3 meter) counts as 5 points; at 2 feet, as 10 points; and at 3 feet (.9 meter), as 15 points. Barrel jumps (laid on their sides) count as 15 points. Point allotments may vary from these somewhat.
 ▸ Penalty for faults and knockdowns is 5 points. Touches or tipped poles do not penalize the rider.
 ▸ Two refusals are permitted; however, on the third refusal the rider will be disqualified.
 ▸ Total scores by adding points of fences successfully jumped and subtracting penalty points for overtime, knockdowns, and the points on a jump that is taken twice or in the wrong direction.

# Cautions

 ▸ Keep the jumps to a 3-foot (.9 meter) maximum.
 ▸ Riders learning to jump may not take 3-foot (.9 meter) or barrel jumps.
 ▸ Plan course carefully to avoid taking sharp turns with speed.

# Variations

 ▸ Offer three courses or allow for three course changes according to riders' abilities. Total points should be figured for various ability levels.
 ▸ Distribute course designs to riders or post a large design in ring.

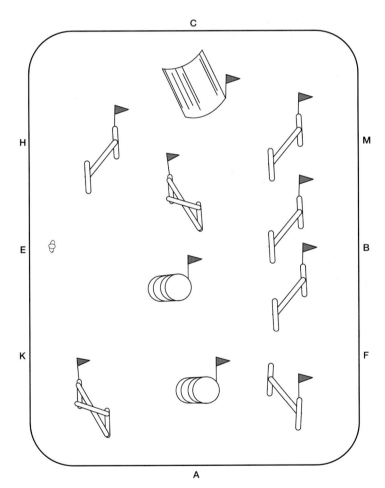

# 39 Maze Jump Course

▶ Advanced Riders Only

Jumps may be taken in any order, as they are not numbered. Having had an opportunity to see only a posted course design, when on the course, riders have little time to plan their routes and may find themselves faced by several jumps with short approaches. Quick, clear, and correct thinking is usually rewarded. Uncertainty can cause a horse to balk at a jump. Because this is a timed event and all jumps must be taken, it can be quite exciting!

### PURPOSE

Challenges riders' memory when faced with a maze of jumps; improves planning, pacing, short rein for quick turns.

# Instructions

1. Set up jumps of various heights in ring arena, each with a red flag or ribbon attached to its right side. (Jumps are to be taken with red flag or ribbon on rider's right.) Start/finish line is established.
2. Instructor signals first rider to begin, starting timer as rider crosses start/finish line.
3. Rider takes all jumps, in any order, but in specified direction (flag or ribbon on rider's right). Once all jumps are taken, rider returns to start/finish line.
4. Instructor stops timer as rider races to start/finish line. A 5-point penalty is given for each refusal, knockdown, or jump with flag on left.
   - **Winner:** Rider with best score; a calm horse/rider combination usually wins.

# Cautions

- Spectators should be advised to stay quiet — no shouting or clapping — as this event requires concentration.
- Make sure jumps do not exceed the ability of the riders. A safe maximum height for jumps in this taxing game is 2 feet (.6 meter).
- Plan course carefully to avoid taking sharp turns with speed.
- Instructors must supervise riders closely to keep horses under control.

# Variations

- Reduce size of jumps.
- Vary type and placement of jumps.
- Run as a group or team, rather than an individual, event.

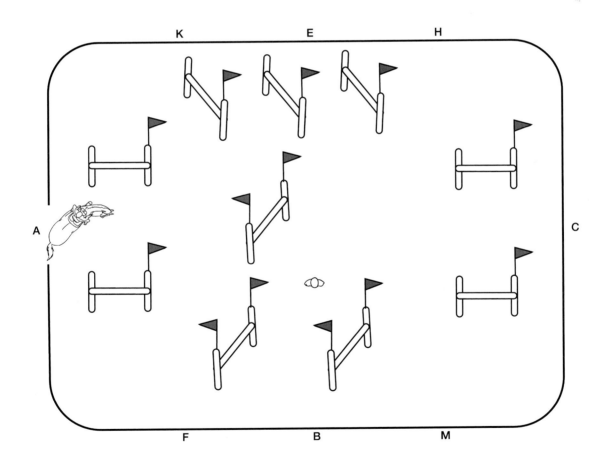

# VII

# Roping Games

Any discussion of roping games requires the use of correct terminology. From the Old English comes the word *rope*, the stout cord of strands or fibers twisted together and used to catch a calf or other critter. The Spanish call it a *lazo*, and we sometimes call it a lasso, lariat, a mecate, or reata. The term used sometimes refers to the material used in the rope. Although in the games that follow we suggest using a cotton clothesline, today most ropes are made of synthetics, which vary in stiffness to better hold a loop, have greater strength, and last longer than ropes made of hemp and other natural materials.

Though exciting and fun, roping games carry a certain amount of risk — specifically, rider and horse may become entangled in the rope. Novice ropers should begin roping stationary objects while standing on the ground, then ty roping stationary objects while mounted. Only when proficiency and skill come should one attempt to rope a moving target. Western cowboys learn to rope at an early age and take good care of that lifeline. Many times, knowledge of roping and a good quality rope have saved the lives of humans and animals. There is tremendous risk of getting fingers caught or pinched when tying off a rope on a saddle, so be careful!

Recently our miniature horse Granny, who is blind in both eyes, wandered into a citrus grower's orange grove. Hundreds of acres of orange trees and deep irrigation canals confounded the poor little horse. After three days of searching, we found her near a deep canal. As we attempted to halter her, she jerked free and slid down the bank into the water. With little more than her head and neck showing, we hurriedly summoned our farrier, a superb roper. He came with his two sons, a hired man, and his wife. One strong rope and a perfectly accurate loop around Granny's neck, which was quickly drawn up to her jaw so as not to choke her, was followed by shouts to "Pull, pull!" It took the combined efforts of four strong people to pull our wet, bedraggled horse to safety, and it was possible only because of the roping expertise of our farrier.

## Equipment Needed for Games

- #10 clothesline
- Hay bales
- Cholla or six small cones secured together with duct tape
- Lime or athletic chalk
- Goal posts, buckets, or jump standards
- Pinnies

◀ Only experienced ropers should be mounted and moving.

# 40 Roping Contest
▶ **Intermediate Riders**

"Little britches" roping contests are common at shows and rodeos, where youngsters rope from the ground, vying for coveted belt buckles. When he was a youngster, our Montana-born instructor competed with his brother by roping the fence posts along the way as they walked to school. They were experts at age eight.

Typically, roping from a horse is a privilege reserved exclusively for teenagers and adults, because of the high risks involved: becoming entangled in the rope and having your horse pulled over by the "ropee" are very serious hazards. Still, roping is exciting and can be great fun.

First you must learn the language of roping. A rope has two ends: the *loop* or "working" end for roping, and the *dally* end that is wrapped, or "tied off," on your saddle horn. The *honda* is the eye at the working end of the rope through which the rope is drawn to form a loop. The *spoke* is the trailing end of rope that is drawn through the honda. (These instructions assume that the bowline knot has been tied and that the roper is right handed and unmounted.)

1. Coil the rope by grasping the dally end firmly in your left hand and drawing the rope around and around, grasping each loop in your left hand as it is formed, until you reach the tied loop end.
2. Grasp the loop and spoke about 2 feet (.6 meters) from the honda.
3. Holding the coils in your left hand and your loop in the right, at ribcage height, open the loop until it almost touches the ground, approximately 4 feet (1.2 meters) across. (With coil hand [left] and loop hand [right] almost completely extended, you should have enough rope to span that distance.)
4. Take the loop almost straight out, swinging hard around and over your head using your wrist. When the loop is in front of you, your thumb should be turned downward to guide the rope; when the loop is over your head, your hand should be palm up and your thumb upturned.
5. When this motion seems comfortable and you have sufficient momentum, lean forward on your right leg, aim, and throw the loop like a football.

# Instructions

1. Purchase #10 clothesline and cut the line into 25- to 30-foot (7.6- to 9.2-meter) lengths for novice ropers. Tie a bowline knot.
2. Have students practice on the ground roping a hay bale, fence posts, or mock heifer made of horns attached to hay bale.
3. Score is kept by an instructor who may give each young cowhand 5 to 10 roping tries on each object. One point is awarded for each object roped.
▸ **Winner:** Person with highest score.

# Cautions

▸ Ground practice is essential!
▸ Do *not* practice roping people!
▸ Horse must be tolerant of rope if roping while mounted.
▸ Do not tie off rope to saddle horn unless the saddle is designed specifically for roping. Roping saddles have stronger saddle "trees" (wood frames) and much stronger, wider girths to accommodate the stress of roping.
▸ Never tie off dally to saddle without the supervision of a competent roper.

# Variations

▸ Rope different objects. Try fence posts, buckets, and goats, to name a few.
▸ While mounted, "park" horse in the center of the ring and attempt to rope an object (e.g., a hay bale) placed nearby. Do not tie off dally end to saddle.
▸ While mounted, walk horse past objects and attempt to rope at the walk.

This rider shows good roping technique: Notice that the thumb is turned downward to guide the rope when the loop is in front.

# 41 Cholla

▶ A d v a n c e d   R i d e r s   O n l y

In the desert a *cholla* (pronounced *choy*-a) is a large cactus. In the riding ring, this cactus is represented by a 2-foot (.6-meter) -high jack, stuffed, and covered with canvas or leather, weighing approximately 15 pounds (6.8 kilograms), with six protruding cones. Cholla is also the name of a roping game. There are usually three riders on each team. Players wear numbers or like-colored shirts for quick identification. A mounted referee may want a stick or pole with a hook on it for easy retrieval of the cholla. This game is similar — in size of field, number of riders, goals, and scoring — to Polo.

If you don't have access to a cholla, secure six small cones together with duct tape for an equally challenging target.

### PURPOSE

Improves hand-eye coordination, balance, teamwork.

# Instructions

1. If a large enough fenced ring is not available, boundaries of game area are marked with lime or athletic chalk on a field. A suitable area is approximately 100 feet by 200 feet (30.5 meters by 61 meters). Set up two goal posts, 25 feet (7.6 meters) apart at each end of playing field. Buckets or some other lightweight, movable objects such as jump standards make good goal posts. The space behind the goals should be 60 feet (18.3 meters) to give the riders room to turn.

2. Riders divide into two teams of three players. Each team is assigned a number: 1, 2, or 3. Like-colored pinnies and team numbers are worn by each team.

3. Referee tosses coin to determine which team goes first, places cholla in center of ring between goals, and signals start of game. Mounted referee gives required signals by whistle and may use a stick with hook to pick up cholla without dismounting.

4. First roper of starting team tries to rope cholla and drag it through team's goal, down the field to opponents' goal, and back through team's goal. Two players from the opposing team try to rope and take away cholla during this "run." If roper is successful, referee signals completion of run and sets up game for first roper on opposing team. The referee may blow whistle at any time to stop game, to regulate play if foul is made, or to disqualify player for poor sportsmanship or poor horsemanship. Players stop immediately on whistle.

5. If run is stopped, referee frees cholla from ropes and signals game to resume from that spot with a free-for-all attack on the cholla. Four riders position themselves 30 feet (9.2 meters) away from cholla and attempt to rope it. Rider who lost cholla and counterpart on opposing team do not participate in free-for-all attack. Any roper who ropes cholla, then drags it through his or her own goal first and then through opponents' goal gets points. Points are scored as listed below.

▸ **Winner:** Team with the most points at the end of six periods.

# Scoring

▸ The highest possible score for a successful run is six points. It is scored per goal in this manner: through first goal is 1 point; through second goal is 2 points; and through third goal is 3 points.

▸ Fouls should be called for the following: Crossing in front of a running horse, coming up to the cholla and trying to rope it from the opposite side, preventing a roper from handling his or her rope, and jerking the cholla while dragging it. Each foul receives 1 to 5 penalty points according to the judgment of the referee. The penalty points are added to the opponents' score.

# Cautions

▸ Always err on the side of safety.

▸ Ropers may not "haze" opponents on the right side (usually their roping side).

▸ No rider may change horses, except in case of accident or if both teams agree to such a change.

# Variation

As an alternative to Cholla, try basketball on horseback or Push Polo — a game in which a large ball is pushed by rider's hand or horse's knee or hoof (see page 114).

The *cholla* is typically made of leather or canvas.

# VIII

# Distance Games

The distance you and your horse travel while playing the games in this section may be as long as 25 miles (40.3 km) or as short as around the ring. Increased distance and challenge are possible as horse and rider acquire better balance, control, and good judgment. Galloping over rough terrain may strain a horse's tendons and ligaments. Holes can trip a horse and send both horse and rider flying. Judgment and safety are learned under supervision in the short distance rides. Always ride on a well-marked trail.

Riding fast is exciting, but sometimes galloping beside another horse may prompt a runaway. To participate in trail rides, riders must know how to circle to slow down and how to avoid hard, slippery ground, mud, frost, and unexpected holes and rocks. Galloping in unknown territory or on a paved road is foolish. In such circumstances, slow to a trot or canter. Deep sand, rolling terrain, and uphill climbs are best negotiated at a jog, trot, or walk. Holes are difficult to see, but you will know if your horse falls into one; fortunately, his other three legs will support him. If riding in the West, keep a wary eye for prairie dog holes. Usually they are so abundant, it's best to skirt the entire area.

Before attempting a distance ride, learn how to take your horse's vital signs. Your horse's breathing can alert you to signs of trouble on the trail. Irregular or fast breathing indicates that he should slow down. Of course, a horse breathes faster when he gallops, just as you do when you run fast in a foot race. Frequent changes of pace will help him recover. As a horse tires, he is inclined to lean on his forehand. To the rider, it will seem that the horse becomes heavier; in addition, it will be more difficult to keep him balanced. Horses are courageous and may want to continue, but the rider must take responsibility for the horse's welfare. Such judgment develops with years of experience, riding many different horses in many different sports.

## Equipment Needed for Games

- First-aid fanny pack or backpack
- Oatmeal or corn
- Toy fox or fox hat
- Horn
- Refreshments

◀ Both horse and rider must be in tip-top shape to participate in distance games, which oftentimes are grueling.

# 42 Ride and Tie Race

▶ **Intermediate Riders**

Runners who enjoy riding will have fun in the sport that has found its way to the Midwest and East from California, where the game was resurrected by Roy Johns in 1971. Johns had read about Ride and Tie, which dates back to 18th-century England, in some literature of the Old West. When a rider lost his horse through gunfire, illness, or lameness, he would often hitch a ride with another horseman. But riding double proved tiring to the horse. So a system was devised whereby one would ride a certain distance, dismount, tie the horse to a bush or tree, and set off on foot. Meanwhile the second rider (now walking) would catch up to the tied horse, mount up, and ride on past

his walking partner. The second rider would ride awhile, find a good tie spot, then dismount, and set off on foot. The horse enjoyed a bit of a rest before the other hombre came along to ride again. In this manner of off-and-on riding, both reached their destination without exhausting the horse.

### PURPOSE

Revive an old survival method from the West; great exercise for "runners" while conserving horse's energy.

# Instructions

1. For youngsters and amateurs, set up a course of 2 to 6 miles (3.2 to 9.7 kilometers) (a large circle with start/finish line is best).
2. Station unmounted staff (or responsible older children) every 100 yards (91.4 meters) or more as "tie spots."
3. Pairs of riders team up with one horse.
4. Instructor announces gait; trot or controlled lope is best.
5. Partners start at same time, one riding to the first tie spot while the other runs. Teams are started at 1-minute intervals. Upon reaching spot, rider dismounts, hands reins to staff member or ties horse, and continues along course on foot.
6. Runner, upon reaching tie spot, retrieves horse from staff member or the post, mounts, and rides along course to next tie spot.
7. Pair moves around course, switching positions at tie spots, until course is completed. Contestants and horse must cross finish line together.
- **Winner:** Team with the best time.

# Tips

- The staff (horse holders) can also help the runners mount.
- Time penalties can be given to those who break the designated gait, usually walk or trot. For each infraction, add 5 seconds to total time.
- Contestants wearing colored shirts or pinnies make the game more watchable for spectators.
- Involve spectators in the race by asking some to work as starter, scorer, timers, horseholders, recorders, announcers, and trail markers. (Timers are needed for each pair.)

# Cautions

- At start, riders should stay 10 to 20 feet (3.1 to 6.1 meters) away from runners.
- Tie horse with a quick-release knot or have halter and rope attached to post.

- For young children, hold the race to a fast trot and provide an outrider to monitor their riding and running for safety.

# Variations

- Ride and Tie Race has many variations. Use your imagination and facilities to make it a fun time for all. Spectators will line the course cheering their favorite team, sometimes offering a cool drink to the foot-sore runner/rider.
- To organize a race for experienced riders or professionals, read Donald Jacobs' book, *Ride and Tie*, published by World Publications, Box 366, Mountain View, California 94042.

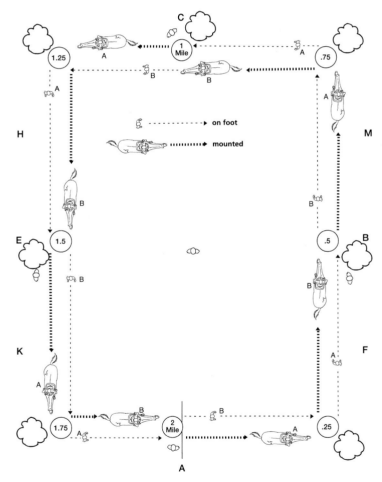

# 43 Hunter Pace

▶ **Advanced Riders Only**

The Hunter Pace lasts about a half day. You can make it a full-day event by setting roads and track warm-up in the morning — like a morning jog on horseback — followed by a lunch and social gathering.

Similar to a trail ride, the course of Hunter Pace is set by organizers and is a timed event that usually includes obstacles such as creek crossings, logs, or low fences to jump. The pace can be somewhat leisurely, depending on the constestant. Some riders enter to win; others enter for the comaraderie.

### PURPOSE

Challenges riders to follow flags or markers for designated course while aiming for an ideal time; encourages courtesy and respect among contestants.

# Instructions

1. Instructor lays out a 3- to 5-mile (4.8- to 8.1-kilometer) course over natural terrain of fields and woods, including 10 to 15 jumps and 5 to 10 spot checks for difficult crossings.
2. Riders form pairs.
3. Instructor announces how winner will be determined: ideal time (pair that finishes closest to average time of all pairs, excluding fastest and slowest times), or posted time (pair that finishes closest to a pre-posted time).
4. Instructor has pairs start out at 3- to 5-minute intervals.
5. When pair arrives at spot checks, horses must take a 5-minute rest if required by organizers. Horses that show signs of excessive strain will be detained until the instructor-judge decides that they are fit to move on. Some rides do not detain riders at spot checks. Riders may deviate from difficult river crossings by riding along bank until shallow crossing area is found.

▸ **Winners:** First pair to cross finish line closest to ideal or posted time.

# Tips

▸ The best posted times are obtained when the instructor or experienced riders complete the course in a responsible manner, allowing for walking time on steep hills, galloping time over flat terrain, and so forth.
▸ If your horse hesitates at the water crossing or at a jump, move aside. Watching other horses negotiating an obstacle without fear or hesitation will likely inspire your horse to do the same. If your horse is still apprehensive, take an alternate route around obstacle.

# Cautions

▸ Remember that Hunter Pace is not a race.
▸ If intermediate-level riders are allowed to participate, they should be well supervised and take alternate routes as needed — around rather than over jumps, for example.
▸ Stay together in small groups, or with at least one partner.

# Variations

▸ There may be categories for novice riders, riders over the fence, on the flat, first time Hunter Pace entries, and by age groups.
▸ If riders are unfamiliar with the area, starting and finishing points are announced well in advance of the event to permit contestants to explore and study the route they wish to ride.
▸ A marked course may be designed over natural country obstacles.

## Checking Vital Signs

- **Pulse** should be 40 beats per minute at rest; an acceptable range is 28–50 beats per minute. Check along inside upper jawbone, temporal artery near back corner of eye, under foreleg, under tail.

- **Respiration** should be 8–12 breaths per minute at rest; an acceptable range is 4–20 breaths per minute. Watch movement of flank or nostril.

- **Capillary refill** determines level of dehydration. Press finger against horse's gum; pink color should return within 1–2 seconds if well hydrated.

# 44 Point-to-Point

▶ **A d v a n c e d   R i d e r s   O n l y**

Point-to-Point evolved from the classic horseback races from one visible steeple to another in a nearby town. Smart horsemen knew that the shorter course was not always the fastest! All competitors start at the same time, often from a "shot gun" start. Point-to-Point is a fast race — not for beginners or the faint of heart.

Designed for skillful riders who race from one point to another point over natural terrain, the distance may be 2 to 5 miles (3.2 to 8.1 kilometers) and the contestants may choose any route. The instructor should select the points so that the shortest route is more difficult, while the longer route presents fewer obstacles, and provides better footing.

Contestants should have time to examine the area if they are not familiar with it. Organizers typically supply maps.

### PURPOSE

Develops independent riding skills; improves horse/rider bond and judgment; challenges riders to discover best and most efficient route.

# Instructions

Instructions are specific to each Point-to-Point. "Spot checkers" are mounted and may hold riders for a 2-minute rest if organizers require one. This may be difficult to enforce if the course is open to any route. A map with all possible routes must show spot checks that riders are required to pass as well as road-crossing hazards.

# Cautions

▸ Some mounted riders may observe the Point-to-Point but are *not allowed* to give advice or directions to other riders. They may assist if a rider or horse falls, however.

▸ Some spot checks are mandatory in order to control riders and ensure saftey.

▸ Do *not* ride alone. Contestants should enter in pairs.

# Variations

▸ If all riders are familiar with the area, do not announce the finish point until all riders are lined up and ready to start!

▸ If riders are unfamiliar with the area, starting and finishing points are announced well in advance of the event to permit contestants to explore and study the route they wish to ride.

▸ A marked course may be designed over natural country obstacles.

Because it is such a demanding event, a 2-minute rest is often required in Point-to-Point.

# 45 Mock Fox Hunt

▶ **Advanced Riders Only**

Our annual mock hunts are the highlight of fall riding. Our mock "master" blows the horn for "rider down" or "fox sighted" or to signal the success of a young rider getting across a deep icy stream! Hot chili after a long afternoon in the field tops off an exciting day. Carry a first-aid fanny pack or back pack and notify local police if crossing busy highways, especially if you have a large group of 20 to 30 riders.

This event is more formal than Hunter Pace, with a "proper attire" protocol and "stirrup cup" (wine for adults, soda for kids) while mounted and when meeting at a designated location.

### PURPOSE

Acquaints rider with hunting terms, protocol, courtesy, adventure, and fun.

# Instructions

1. Organizers mark trail with 1-foot (.3-meter) -long trail of oatmeal spaced about 30 to 50 feet (9.2 to 15.3 meters) apart. (The trail can be colored for different groups or a group may use corn, corn cobs, oats, or local feed that will be picked up by birds.) Course may go over fences or along fields. Trail should be at least 1 mile (1.6 kilometers) long, preferably 2 or 3 miles (3.2 or 4.8 kilometers). The "finish line" is the "fox" — perhaps a papier-mâché replica.
2. Hunt begins and riders follow trail to fox. Mounted fox may move around his den, trying to elude riders. If sighted, fox may return to den.
3. Once fox is located, the master's horn gives several long blasts to announce location. This summons groups to the area.
4. Groups describe their hunt, terrain, obstacles, and adventure.
   - **Winner:** Group to arrive first at "fox den."

# Tips

- If a human "fox" is not available, set a toy fox under a tree or post a "fox den" sign.
- Field master should identify horn blasts prior to ride to acquaint riders with "ware hole" ("beware of the hole"; one blast), rider down (two blasts), and completion (three or more blasts).
- Riders should dress appropriately for anticipated weather.

# Cautions

- Riders should never ride alone. Always stay with at least one other rider.
- Safety first!

# Variations

- Several groups of riders may start out on separate trails, laid out as described previously, with all the trails converging on the "fox." The first group of riders to reach the fox is the winning team. You need a large area in which to lay several trails so that they do not cross each other. If you do not have 100 acres (40.5 hectares) or more, you may lay cross trails, using different colored substances that birds and small animals will eat later. Also, you can add some food coloring to the oatmeal.
- Divide riders into two groups: one group of experienced riders to take the fences, while the novice riders take a course on the flat. Arrange to meet at a creek crossing or prearranged spot for a brief rest and the traditional "stirrup cup," usually at completion. Refreshments for young riders can be apple cider or hot chocolate. Both groups can then join together, hunt, and move on into new terrain that has been approved by the landowner. It's likely that the riders will spot deer, possibly fox and other wild creatures. Hunt courtesy and protocol can be taught along the way.

# IX

# Polo Games

Polo became popular in England in the 1870s and arrived in America in the 1880s. Speed, stamina, precision, courage, and control of the mount are vital in polo. Team members may pass the ball to each other at full speed, requiring sharp twists and turns. The rules dictate that all riders use the right hand regardless of preference. Played at an almost continuous gallop, polo is extremely exciting and tires even the fittest ponies and players.

A word about ponies — in polo, the term signifies any mount, not necessarily an equine under 14.2 hands. Most "ponies" are Thoroughbreds of 15.3 hands or more in height. Today, the best polo ponies are bred in Argentina — a combination of the small ranch horse and the Thoroughbred, usually standing around 15.2 to 15.3 hands. Even if they aren't the ideal size, most riding school horses or camp horses can play a good game of polo. Their generous, adaptable nature allows them to be ridden by many different people, and this flexibility makes them particularly well suited to polo.

Polo can be fun at the walk, trot, or canter. No matter the speed, accuracy in maneuvering and shooting is far more important. Connecting mallet to ball with a long, smooth swing, or passing the ball to a teammate in scoring position is at the heart of the game. As in any game, to be played well, the rules of polo must be observed by all. For the sake of safety and good sportsmanship, all players also must respect the referee. Serious accidents can occur with rough riding or riding in front of a player to cut him off — a grave foul. The referee works to safeguard horse and rider.

Many types of polo exist. Choose the game that best suits you or, better, design your own game and create your own rules. Consider the similarity of polo to other ball games: football, soccer, and basketball to name a few. Where do you think those games came from? Some people think they all started with polo!

## Equipment Needed for Games

- Large ball
- Buckets
- Cones
- Brooms
- Masking tape/ electrical tape
- Bamboo fishing pole
- Broom handle
- Tennis ball
- Lime or baseball diamond chalk
- Polo mallet
- Polo ball
- Polocrosse racket
- Goalposts

◀ An exciting sport for riders, horses, and spectators, polo demands precision and excellent maneuvering.

# 46 Push Polo

▶ **Intermediate Riders**

Push Polo helps acquaint horses with balls so that they are unafraid of them at a real polo match. In Push Polo, the ball must be sufficiently large so the horse cannot avoid it — a large rubber ball or the popular horse ball play toy (the handle can be taped down if necessary) works well. Polo mallets or brooms are not needed for this particular game. Instead, riders try to get their horses to push the ball through the goal. It's surprising how far and how fast horses can push! Even so, when the game is played for the first time, horses do well just to get the ball to the other end of the ring. Riders are allowed to reach down with their hands to push the ball or to kick it with their feet. It definitely helps to have long legs and to be mounted on a short horse!

Beginners can enjoy this game with horses who have been conditioned for pushing a ball. The walk is the best gait for beginners.

### PURPOSE

Acquaints horse with and conditions horse to ball; improves rider's reining ability.

# Instructions

1. Two buckets or cones are placed about 12 to 20 feet (3.6–6.1 meters) apart at one end of ring to define the goal. Start line is established at opposite end of ring.
2. Riders break into teams.
3. Instructor designates gait: walk/trot.
4. Riders move their horses to ball and horses push ball with their legs or noses.

▶ **Winner:** First team to score goal, or team to score the most goals within set time frame.

# Cautions

▶ Use fairly solid balls, *not* inflated balls that will explode if stepped on.
▶ Instructors *must* acquaint/condition horses to ball before play begins.

▶ Because horses are in close contact, they must get along well — no kickers!
▶ Instructors must closely observe horse body language to safeguard novice players.

# Variations

▶ Once horses become accustomed to the large ball, introduce a slightly smaller ball for an even greater challenge. Continue to introduce smaller balls as horses become proficient.
▶ Try this game bareback! For novice horses, riders may use feet or hands to get the ball rolling.
▶ Once horses understand what is expected, set a "no hands" and "no feet" rule for riders — only the horse should move the ball.

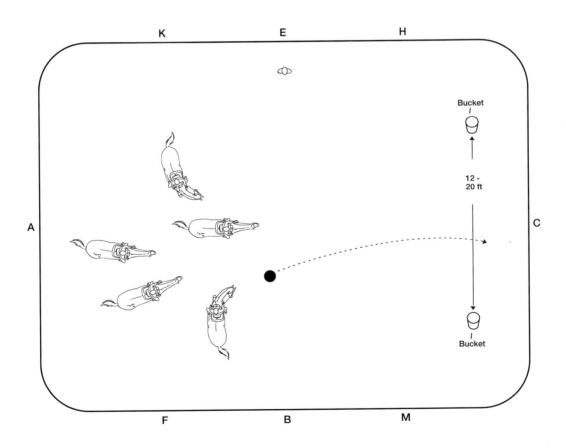

# 47 Broom Polo
▶ Intermediate Riders

Play Broom Polo with two teams of three or four riders each. Use old brooms — be sure to wrap bristles with masking or electrical tape to make them stronger and less flexible — or broomsticks or bamboo fishing poles cut to about 48 or 50 inches (122–127 centimeters). For the mallet end on a broomstick or bamboo pole, cut a slit in an old tennis ball and insert the stout end of the stick or pole all the way into the ball. Binding the ball to the pole with electrical tape helps keep everything together. These mallets tend to last a lot longer than brooms and are not dangerous for riders or horses.

The walk/trot is suggested for riders new to this game; the canter also works well but is not suggested for a small field of less than 200 feet (61 meters).

### PURPOSE

Improves accuracy in reining, balance, teamwork; safe introduction to real polo.

# Instructions

1. Two buckets are placed about 12 to 20 feet (3.6–6.1 meters) apart and at least 10 feet (3 meters) from each end of ring.
2. Riders divide into two teams of three or four players. Riders are assigned numbers 1, 2, 3, or 4 and line up in order on their horses side by side. Riders wear pinnies with big numbers to help identify position and teams.
3. First riders of each team line up facing each other, near center line of ring.
4. The umpire bowls a 12-inch (30-centimeter) diameter ball between opposing teams at center line.
5. Both first players attempt to hit ball toward their goal.
6. The second players move up to follow through if their teammate misses ball. The third players defend opponents' goal. The fourth player (usually the weakest rider) stays out of the fray, hoping to follow up with a good shot or to defend goal.
7. The first three positions rotate after each *chukker* (7-minute play period), with first player defending the goal and third player moving into second player's position and so on. This assures every player a piece of the action.

▶ **Winner:** First team to acquire 10 points, or team to have most points at the end of 6 chukkers.

# Tips

▶ Add a "wrist hold" to mallet or stick, using an inch-wide strap. This lessens the chance of "flying" shots.
▶ Mark field off carefully with lime.
▶ For players new to Broom Polo, it is easier to play a game to 10 points. This eliminates the need for a timer. A 10-point game generally takes 40 to 60 minutes including the time-out for rest, ball out of bounds, and so forth.

▶ Instructor should call fouls for any maneuver that appears to be dangerous to another rider or horse. A very obvious foul occurs when a rider cuts in front of a player who is pursuing the ball. Fouls are called for striking an opponent's horse; backing up a horse to get a better swing at the ball; swinging in front of, beneath, or above an opponent's mount; or just standing over the ball.
▶ When there is an infraction of the rules, the fouled team gets a free shot. Place the ball directly in front of the goal, about 40 to 50 feet (12.2–15.3 meters) away. A player rides unopposed to the ball for the free shot, and as soon as the swing is completed, play resumes. In all polo games, when the player misses a shot, he must ride away from the ball, allowing others to take a shot.
▶ When the ball goes out of bounds, it should be tossed in at that point by an umpire, spectator, or assistant. Riders should halt when the ball goes out of bounds. Riders resume motion as soon as the ball is tossed back in.
▶ The size of the playing field depends on the size of the facilities. The smaller the field, the slower the gait at which the game should be played.

# Cautions

▶ Accustom horses to the sound of the mallet or broom hitting an inflated ball.
▶ If regulation mallets are used, wrap the horses' legs to prevent injury to the cannon bone.

# Variation

Experienced, intermediate riders can use regulation mallets instead of brooms or fishing poles.

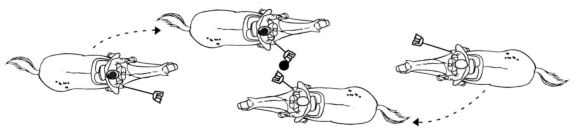

Polo is a team sport — keep your horse moving, and don't stand around.

# 48 Polo Skill Tests

▶ Advanced Riders Only

**PURPOSE**

Develop and refine fundamental polo skills
in individual and team settings.

Many of the skills needed to play polo successfully
can be tested in individual practice or competitions.
Following is a very basic game to develop basic
mallet-handling skills, as well as a few tried-and-true
suggestions for practice on horseback. Be patient
when first starting out — comfort, confidence, and
skill come with time — and have fun!

**PURPOSE**

Develop and refine fundamental polo skills
in individual and team settings.

# Instructions

1. Holding polo mallet, stand on a firm bench or chair (approximately 24 inches [61 centimeters] high).
2. Instructor or assistant, who is also unmounted, stands between two cones or markers about 10 to 20 feet (3.1 to 6.1 meters) away from player on chair.
3. Instructor or assistant rolls ball toward player on chair.
4. Player on chair attempts to drive or hit ball to cone or marker at left or right of assistant.

▸ **Winner:** Player to hit the ball closest to the marker.

# Variations

▸ **Triple Hit** — Skill test for rider in which rider has three chances to hit the ball. Rider who hits ball farthest from the start line wins.

▸ **Single Back Shot** — Skill test for rider, who has one chance to hit ball as far as possible with back shot. Back shot may be made from off side or near side, as designated.

▸ **Polo Pony Race** — A 50-yard dash from a standing start. Each rider has a different-colored ball and must hit it through goalposts, cones, or buckets, as designated. Excellent practice for an individual or from two to four riders. Winner is first to hit ball to finish line. *Caution:* Do *not* cut in front of other riders.

▸ **Polo Bucket Race** — Two buckets are set 20 to 40 or 60 yards (18.3–36.6 or 54.8 meters) apart. Rider works his ball to bucket at gait designated, hits it around bucket, then returns to start/finish line. Tests speed and ability of pony and accuracy of rider. A winning time is around 30 seconds on a field 100 to 120 yards (91.4–110 meters) long.

▸ **Team Relay** — Players work in pairs — one takes only off-side shots, while partner takes only near-side shots. Team moves ball from player to player up the field toward the goal. First ball through the goal wins (two pairs can play, each pair with their own ball). Players change sides (from near side to off side and vice versa) after each goal outdoors. Change at the end of a chukker when played indoors.

▸ **Paddock Polo** — Played in a fenced arena, in this game the ball is hit against the board fence (paddock), bounces off, and is retrieved by teammate (much like squash or billiards.) There are three players for each team, and an inflated ball is used. First team to move the ball across goal line wins.

Good hand-eye coordination and control are essential to making a winning shot.

# 49 Polocrosse

▶ **A d v a n c e d   R i d e r s   O n l y**

The purely Australian horse sport of polocrosse derives from an equestrian exercise in England. Polocrosse was first introduced in the United States by students at Lake Erie College in Painesville, Ohio, who had been to Australia as part of Academic Terms Abroad to play and study polocrosse. This sport combines a love of competition and horses, and offers a chance to play a horse sport that requires only one horse per player. Polocrosse has grown quickly in the United States because it's a family sport: It's for all ages and can be enjoyed at different levels. (For more information on polocrosse, write the American Polocrosse Association, P.O. Box 853, Johnson City, TX 78636.)

As the name implies, polocrosse is a combination of polo and lacrosse played on horseback. Each rider is equipped with a cane — a polo-mallet shaft to which is attached a squash-racket head having a loosely twisted thread net. The stick may be any length, usually from 3 to 4 feet (.9 to 1.2 meters) overall. The ball is made of a thick-skinned sponge rubber that is 4 inches (10.2 centimeters) in diameter and weighs approximately 6 ounces (170 grams).

Each player is permitted only one horse in a match or tournament; however, a substitute may be played if a horse is injured. Ideal horse height is between 14 and 16 hands.

# The Teams

Each team consists of six mounted players, divided into two sections of three, that play alternate *chukkers*, or time periods. Six or eight chukkers usually constitute a full match. Each chukker is 6 to 8 minutes long (determined by the tournament committee), with a 2-minute break between chukkers. This gives an 8- or 10-minute rest period for the section not in play. In each section, the three players are number 1, or attacker; number 2, or center, and number 3, or defender. The attacker is the only player who can score a goal for the team, but only from the goal-scoring area (see field diagram). The center, usually the pivot player on the team, can only play in the center of the field, while the defender is the only player who can defend the team's goal.

# Equipment

In addition to the polocrosse stick and ball, in American Polocrosse Association–sanctioned tournaments players are required to wear a suitable helmet, white pants, team color shirts, and proper boots. Horses are outfitted in polo bandages and bell boots on all four legs. A breast collar must be worn.

# The Game

The game is played on a field 160 yards (146 meters) long and 60 yards (54.8 meters) wide, but fewer riders can play in a smaller riding ring. (Playing-field dimensions can be altered to suit the ability level of riders and available space.) The penalty lines that enclose the goal-scoring area are 30 yards (27.4 meters) from either end of the field. The ball must be bounced or passed over this penalty line and any player carrying the ball over will incur a penalty. The goalposts are set 8 feet (2.4 meters) apart at either end of the field and are enclosed by an 11-yard (10.1-meter) semicircle. Goals must be attempted from within the goal-scoring area but outside of the 11-yard (10.1-meter) goal circle. The combined total of goals by both sections within a team determines the winning score.

The game begins in center field, the players lining up side by side, with the attacker in front, the center next, and the defender in the back. The ball is thrown in by the mounted umpire, high and above the players' heads. Whenever an attempt at a goal fails, the defender throws the ball back into play from just behind the penalty line, at a point directly in front of where the ball crossed the back line. The throw must cover 10 yards (9.1 meters) in any direction, and all other players must keep the line free.

Players carrying the ball in their net may only carry it on their "stick-side." For example, a right-handed player carries the ball on the right, or offside of the player's horse, but can pick it up or catch it on the left, or "non-stick" side, provided that the net is immediately brought back to the stick side. All players can pick up the ball, catch it in their nets, or pass it to a teammate. Only the attacker can shoot a goal. Hitting at an opponent's stick, called "giving wood," is permitted, either to dislodge the ball or to prevent the opponent from gaining possession of the ball, as long as it is done with an upward motion. Hitting down constitutes a foul. Dangerous swings can result in a free goal to the opposition. Bumping at an angle or bumping with sufficient force to dislodge a horse bodily from its line of travel is dangerous to horse and rider. Crossing, stopping on the ball, and elbowing are fouls. The wedging of one player between two other players is also a foul. The penalty for such fouls is a free throw to the opposing team from a spot designated on the field by the mounted umpire.

# Cautions

Safety comes first! Follow rules and respect the umpire to ensure that riders and horses are safe at all times. Riders unable to do this should not play.

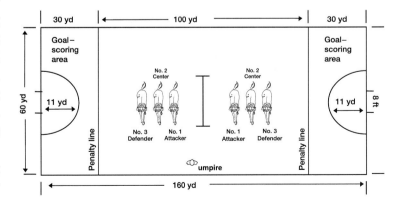

# X

# Mounted Drills

A mounted drill provides considerable interest and variety for riders and horses while at the same time providing exercise. The drill requires alertness, attention, and prompt action on the part of both rider and horse, along with precision, timing, cooperation, and coordination. A well-designed drill offers a kaleidoscope of color and movement — it provides an entertaining show for spectators and can be an exciting prelude to other events.

The drill may be conducted by a series of voice or hand commands, by whistle signals, or the drill may be memorized. When drills are orally executed, use a *command of preparation* followed by a command of execution. When hand signals are used (see p. 133) by the drill leader, allow sufficient time for preparation and execution. Be sure to practice before the drill. If anything goes wrong, the lead rider must guide the team out of the confusion by leading them off in a straight line or large circle, whichever is easiest. Someone is bound to get mixed up, so try to keep it lighthearted and fun.

The drill can be performed to music. Select a military march or a popular hit suited to the gait you'll be using. You'll need 4/4 time for the walk, 2/4 time for the trot, and 6/8 time for the canter. Musical drills can help riders with pacing, the music cuing them to what will happen when. A battery-operated tape deck works best, as power is not always available ringside.

While it's nice to drill horses of proximate size, initially horses should be matched by temperament. Later, pairs can be matched by color and size, so that they have approximately the same length of stride.

With enough time, practice, and patience, you can pull it all together. Coordinating riders' dress; the size, stride, and color of horses; and adding splashes of complementary colors in leg wraps, saddle pads, and flags accentuate the precision of the horses' movements.

Most drills look best when done in the sitting trot or the canter. Young children and novice drill team members should walk the drill on foot and on horseback several times before attempting to trot or canter.

◀ When well executed, mounted drills are exciting to watch. Alertness, attention, and prompt action are required of both horse and rider.

# 50 Mounted Drill Team

▶ Intermediate Riders

Riders of any age can improve their horsemanship by riding in a drill team. Drilling, like any team sport, requires cooperation, precision, keenness, and self-discipline. Drilling is not only good for the riders but excellent for the horses. Both enjoy the challenge of working together to develop harmony and beauty in a synchronized sport.

Simple, basic drill routines are best for youngsters. The following series of drills is a good pattern to present to beginners. Before they begin, pairs of riders should work together at the walk and the trot, executing circles, half circles, halts, and transitions. One of the riders should be the designated leader,

directing his or her partner to increase or decrease the pace as needed. Usually the outside rider of the pair is the pacesetter, because the outside rider has farther to go when cornering and in circles; the inside rider needs to slow down a bit to keep pace.

### PURPOSE

Develops precision and accuracy in movement; promotes teamwork.

# Instructions

1. Riders divide into pairs, then line up in single column of eight at end of ring.
2. Instructor gives preparatory command, "Column of twos," followed 3 seconds later by "Column of twos — ho."
3. Riders join their partners, ride down center in pairs to opposite end of ring, then divide right and left.

## Figure Eight (Thread-the-Needle)

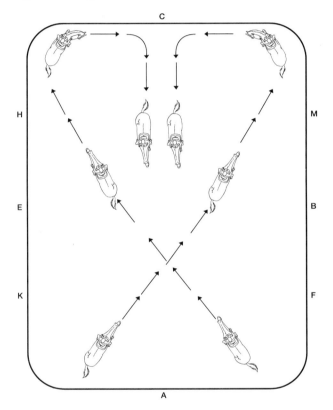

1. Riders proceed toward center (**X**) at a diagonal, glancing to partner across width of ring, keeping steady pace. Outside rider of pair crosses in front at **X** and is considered the leader or pacesetter in all maneuvers.
2. Riders proceed to corners of arena, then move toward center of short wall (**C**). They rejoin to turn down center as a pair. When they reach the opposite end (**A**), pairs separate.
3. Pairs repeat Figure Eight to get back to original position.

## Crossover

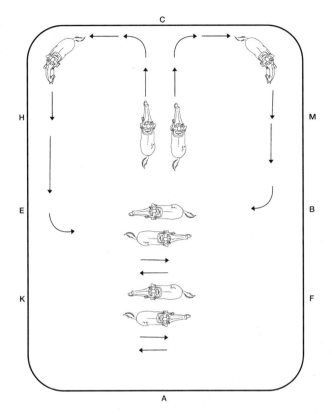

1. Pairs turn down center at **A**, divide right and left at **C**, and continue along long walls of ring.
2. Instructor gives preparatory command, "Prepare crossover" and specifies that riders are to cross right leg–to–right leg.
3. Pairs cross from one side of arena to other, passing their partners at center line of the arena, right leg–to–right leg.
4. Riders return to single column, riding around edge of arena or riding a large circle following the leader. Riders should be about 4 feet (1.2 meters) apart, or even head to tail.

## Snail

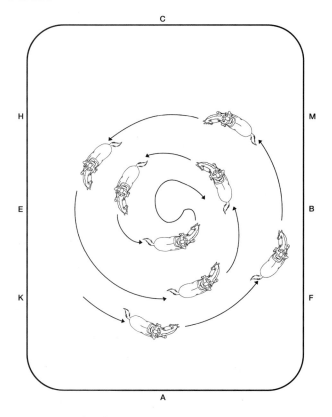

1. Lead rider leads team in circular pattern.
2. After completing one or more nearly perfect circles, lead rider moves gradually into center of revolving riders, leading them into a smaller circle.
3. When there is no more room to circle, lead rider turns in opposite direction and leads team out of circle.

## Tricycle

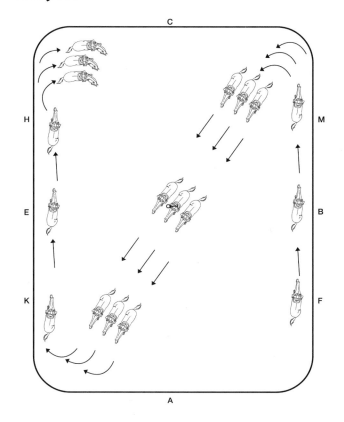

1. Single column of riders tracks along the long wall.
2. When riders reach corner, first three riders turn horses sharply toward diagonal and line up three abreast. All horses' noses are even as riders continue across diagonal. The remaining riders form in threes and follow the lead threesome.
3. Upon reaching opposite corner, riders slip apart into single column and track in opposite direction from which they began tricycle.
4. Riders repeat pattern two or four times, positioning lead rider back into original place as head of column.

# Tips

- Using a dressage arena as shown or marking the fence with letters will help the riders become more accurate in their turns and circles.
- Keep all commands and directions clear and concise. Any clutter adds confusion and uncertainty. The leader, therefore, must understand the movements and know exactly what has to happen. Work out all the patterns on paper beforehand.
- A few reminders for riders when doing the Snail: Riders should shorten their reins to gain control in these tight circles. When horses are in close quarters, some may be inclined to take a kick at a neighbor. Allow enough room between horses so that the lead rider coming out of the circle is not crunched by the oncoming horses. The Snail for eight riders is exciting and not too difficult. With twelve or more riders, it is spectacular!

In Crossover, good timing and proper spacing are essential.

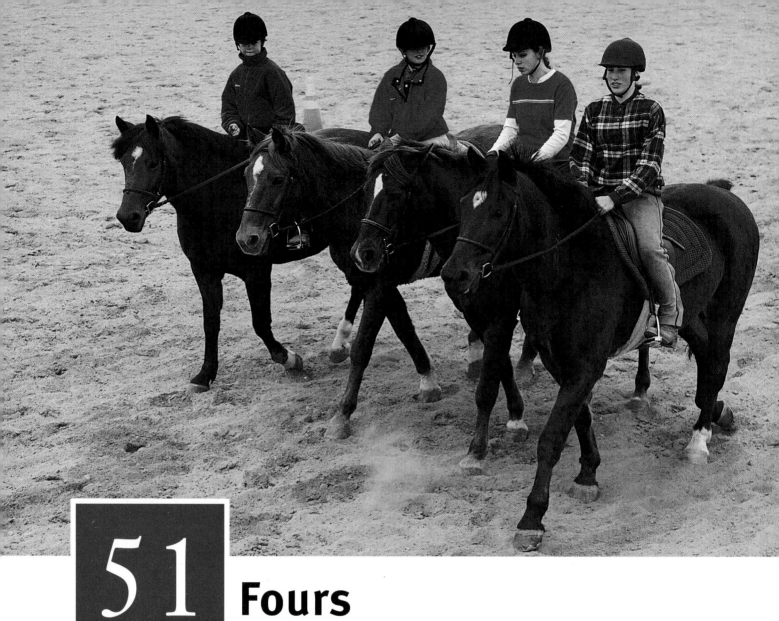

# 51 Fours

▶ **Intermediate Riders**

Four horses abreast, moving in synchrony, is a thrill for riders and spectators. Many of the maneuvers done by twos can also be executed by fours. After working out the simple patterns of circles, serpentines, figure eights, pairs, and threes, everyone wants to try fours. The lead rider on the outside retains that position in fours and advises his or her team to slow down or catch up, as the case may be. It takes a lot of practice to keep the harmony and synchronization of the drill.

# Instructions

1. Riders divide into pairs, then line up in single column of eight at **A**, end of ring.
2. Instructor gives preparatory command, "Column of twos," followed 3 seconds later by "Column of twos — ho."
3. Riders join their partners at **A**, ride down center in pairs to opposite end of ring, then turn left.
4. Pair number one remains on the outside near the wall while pair number two moves up on the inside.
5. Instructor gives preparatory command, "Column of fours," followed 3 seconds later by "Column of fours — ho."
6. When fours approach each corner, lead rider and partner speed up, permitting inside pair to retain same pace.
7. As riders come out of corner and onto long wall, outside pair slackens pace. This permits inside pair to retain the same pace all the way around the ring.

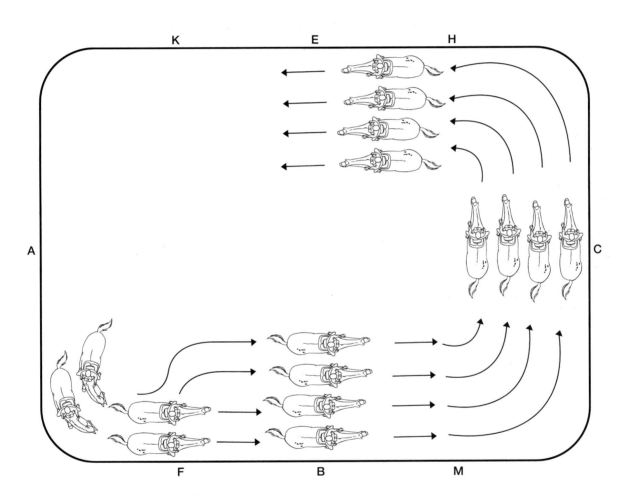

# 52 More Advanced Drills

▶ **Advanced Riders Only**

This pattern of drills ends with a twelve-horse pinwheel. A spectator pleaser, the twelve-horse pinwheel requires considerable practice to keep correct timing and spacing. Quite often the middle riders get squeezed into retreating or advancing out of the line! On completion of the pinwheel, troop may halt, salute the cheering audience, and canter out of the ring in fours or a single column. (A large ring, at least 66 feet [20.1 meters] wide, is needed for the twelve-horse pinwheel.)

# Instructions

1. Riders line up in column of twos and divide at A, moving in single columns right and left.
2. When all riders are on long wall, they simultaneously execute individual circles of about 20- to 30-feet (6- to 10-meters) in diameter, depending on size of arena.
3. Riders rejoin partners at C, move down center line, and divide right and left at A.
4. When all riders are on long walls opposite each other, they execute half circle returning to track and moving in opposite direction.
5. Riders repeat half circle so that lead riders are once again in lead. (Half circle will place the last pair temporarily in the lead.) *Note:* If riders are skilled in dressage, this is most beautifully done as a turn on the haunches.

## Pinwheels

1. First and second sets of fours pinwheel to the left, full circle.
2. When returning to centerline, second set of fours pinwheels to the right with third set of fours.
3. All halt on centerline, then peel off in fours to the left. Fours circle ring.
4. On long wall, all three sets of fours simultaneously turn to center, halting on centerline (all facing the same direction).
5. All twelve horses pinwheel, circling to the left. Inside two riders will turn on the forehand while outside riders are cantering on the wheel.

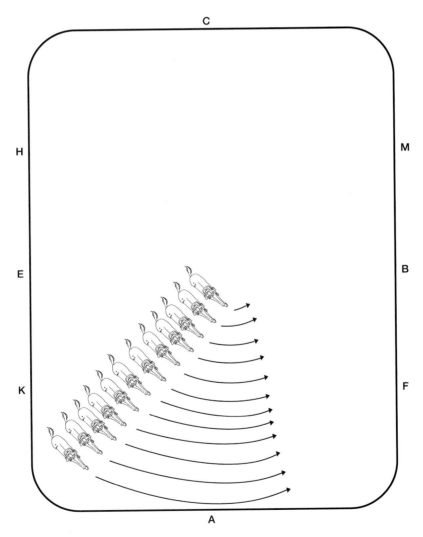

# 53 Cavalry Drill or Flag Drill

▶ Advanced Riders Only

This event requires approximately 4 hours of practice — preferably in half hour sessions — to reach a desirable precision. The drill itself, when the desired standard of precision is reached, should last about 20 minutes; it can be shortened to 10 minutes and — with a little repetition — can be increased to 30 minutes.

Eight to twenty-four riders are needed to perform the drill in a regular-size ring. If the space is available, the number might be increased to thirty-six or even forty-eight. More than forty-eight riders require an open field; the field can be marked with lime for practice, but this probably won't be necessary once riders understand the drill. Drill teams larger than forty-eight would probably be unwieldy and very difficult to control, even if the riders and horses were experienced. However, remember that horses are herd animals and enjoy moving together. Anything is possible! Practice drills in groups of eight, then put groups together for a fantastic drill.

A military-type drill follows. Amplification and modifications are easily applied to correspond to the ability and experience of the group and its leader. The term "march" may be replaced by "ho." Commands are given verbally by leader.

Fall in.

Count fours. Anyone who feels incapable of riding at positions 1 or 4 (inside and outside), change positions.

Fours right, march.

Column right, march.

Column of twos, march.

Column of riders, march.

Trot, march.

Column of twos, march.

Column of fours, march.

Column of riders, march.

Change hands. (At the next corner, the column moves diagonally across the arena and changes direction.)

Walk, march.

Release stirrups.

Slow trot, march (once around ring).

Walk, march.

Half-turn.

Riders circle to the left.

Half-turn and reverse.

Half-turn.

Riders circle to the right.

Half-turn and reverse.

Take stirrups.

From front to rear count threes.

Trot, march.

By threes, by the left flank, march. (Track right at end of arena.)

Column of fours, march.

Walk, march.

Riders, halt.

Column of fours from the right. Trot, march.

Column right, march.

Column of twos, march.

Column of riders, march.

(At the middle of one end of the ring) Column right, march.

(At opposite end of ring) Riders left and right.

Columns half left and half right (When leading riders on each side reach end of ring. This produces a crossover or crisscross in the center of the ring).

(At end of ring) Column of twos.

Twos, left and right.

(Twos) Columns half left and half right (crisscross).

(Twos) Columns half left and half right (Double back).

(At end of ring) Column of fours.

Fours, left and right.

(Fours) Columns half left and half right (crisscross).

(Fours) Columns half left and half right (Double back).

(Caution — "Even fours left, odd fours right.")

(At end of ring) Line, march.

Walk, march.

Riders, halt.

Lead out from the right and ride at will — cool your horses.

Assemble

Forward

Fours

Fours right

Ho          Halt

# Variation

This drill can be adapted to any theme, such as Western Square Dance, Grand Old Flag, Westward Ho, or use a local theme with representative costumes. Use terms appropriate to costumes.

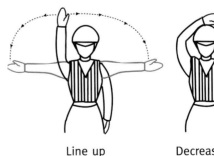

Line up          Decrease gait

# Appendix

## Competitive Trail Rides

Popular nationwide, competitive trail rides are generally 25 miles long. The goal of the ride is not to cross the finish line first, but rather to maintain your horse in the best possible physical condition throughout the ride. Veterinarians and assistants who are skilled in taking horses' pulse and respiration readings judge the riders — not the clock.

### Veterinary Check

A pre-ride briefing and veterinary check are done approximately 1 hour before the ride begins. The veterinary check establishes the normal pulse and respiration rate of the horse at rest, which is recorded. Veterinarians also assess soundness and general condition. The pre-ride briefing by the organizers informs riders as to trail conditions, route, and miles of the ride. This is very important, as riders may not school their horses on the trail prior to the ride. Obviously, a well-marked trail is equally important.

Halfway through the ride, veterinarians will check each horse during a mandatory half-hour rest stop. Ten minutes after the rider and horse arrive at the rest stop the horse's pulse and respiration will be checked and recorded. The horse is also checked for lameness, dehydration, and abrasions. Rules usually stipulate that riders take complete care of their horses (i.e., water, feed, and groom) at rest stops and post-ride checks. Horses in good condition may continue on the ride.

There usually is a surprise checkpoint along the route. The horse is quickly checked by the veterinarian-judge, who allows the rider to continue if the horse is in satisfactory condition.

The veterinarians again give a thorough examination to the horses at the end of the ride. The winners are determined by averaging each horse's pulse and respiration readings and determining which horses have completed the ride in the best condition.

### Gait

The most frequently used gait is a 6- to 8-miles per hour (9.7- to 12.9-kilometers per hour) trot. A good ground-covering stride, the trot is less fatiguing for the horse. In a 25-mile (40.3-kilometer) ride, the time allowed is usually 3 to 3½ hours. Time is not counted at mandatory rest stops of ½ to ¾ hour or at surprise vet checks. Steep hills, roads, and water crossings may slow the progress of the riders; road crossings are often monitored by unmounted assistants.

### Ride Level

Riders usually cover the marked trails in groups. There is great camaraderie on the rides, with opportunities for conversing and giving helpful hints to novices. Rides are divided for novices and experienced riders. Novice rides are sometimes 10 to 13 miles (16.1 to 21 kilometers) on fairly level terrain with no road or water crossings. For Level II intermediate riders (those who can walk, trot, and canter and show good control and good horsemanship), 10 to 15 to 25 miles (16.1 to 24.2 to 40.3 kilometers) of somewhat challenging terrain is a good length. Level III advanced riders may travel from 25 to 100 miles (40.3 to 161.3 kilometers) on varied terrain.

## Ride Distance

Organizers may hold a 25-mile (40.3-kilometer) ride on one day and a 50- or 100-mile (80.7- or 161.3-kilometer) endurance ride on the same weekend. Participants often arrive a day before the ride and camp out with the horses.

## Riding Tips

For camp or riding-school participants, use trail-wise horses, mark trails carefully, and have experienced staff observe or accompany the riders. Mounted staff may be assigned at checkpoints along the way.

Horses with a tendency to kick should have a red ribbon braided into their tail to notify others to keep a safe distance. When passing, tell the rider you are "passing on the left (or right)" in a clear voice.

**Uphill/Downhill.** When riding uphill, rest your hands on the mane or neck and stand in balance, allowing the horse to use his quarters to push him uphill. It is easier to ride downhill when sitting tall and straight, using frequent checks and releases to monitor the horse's speed. Always ride straight downhill, as horses tend to slip easily going sideways. Their lateral balance is poor.

**Mud/Streams.** Move slowly through muddy areas and streams. Horses sometimes like to roll in a stream. You prevent an attempt to lie down by pulling up slightly on the reins when you feel the horse's knees sag slightly.

**Hazards.** Call out to riders behind you when you see any hazards, such as holes, wire, and so forth. All riders appreciate courtesy on the trail. When a rider stops to remove a jacket or tighten a girth, wait until the rider has remounted before proceeding. Horses do not like to be left behind and may rush to catch up, leaving the rider behind.

**Roads/Traffic.** When riding along roads with automobile traffic, stay in single file off the pavement. Traffic laws vary from state to state as to which side of the road horses should be on. In general it is best to move with the oncoming traffic, rather than have trucks or cars come up suddenly from behind. When crossing a road, riders should cross as one body, at a walk. The safest way to cross is a flank turn, or riders can dismount and lead their horses across, again using the flank turn.

## Rules

Some of the general rules followed by the Upper Midwest Endurance and Competitive Ride Association are:

▸ The ride is open to all breeds.
▸ On a 25-mile (40.3-kilometer) ride the horses must be at least 4 years old.
▸ The ride must be controlled by veterinarians.
▸ Any type tack is permissible.
▸ The same horse and rider must pass all checkpoints in the designated order and must stay on the marked trail. Ride organizers may make changes if the trail or weather conditions warrant it; however, any changes must be announced prior to the ride.
▸ Protective headgear is not mandatory, but it is recommended for all riders. Horses tend to become excited in strange territory, shying from common objects such as signs and mailboxes.

In competitive trail rides, it is best to ride with experienced horses, who are able to instill confidence in the novice horse or rider. Remember that a competitive trail ride is not a race, although some riders and their mounts would like to make it so. Moderate pace, courtesy to others, and sensible riding help ensure safety.

For more information on safe horsemanship practices, contact
    Horsemanship Safety Association
    P.O. Box 2710
    Lake Placid, FL 33862-2710
    tel: 800-798-8106
    fax: 941-699-5577
    e-mail: hsanews@juno.com

*Storey Books extends a special thank you to Carol DeMayo, Lisa DeMayo, and the student riders at DeMayo's Bonnie Lea Farm in Williamstown, Massachusetts, for their cooperation and assistance in capturing the spirit of these games in print.*

Pictured from left to right are *(top)* Danielle Roy, Ali Wassick, Ali Guerin, Sophie Kohut, Sarah Gatling, Howard Morrison, Britt Johnson, and Jessie Masters; *(middle)* Brittany Bullett, Ashley McLeod, Samantha Halek, "Bubba," Lisa DeMayo, Hannah Giroux, and Katlynn LeMaire; *(bottom)* Jessica Hill, Karolyn Maloney, Ali Bona, Carol DeMayo, "Hannah," Mark Maselli, Miranda Bona, and "Tucker." Not pictured are Kelsey Chandler, Mark Chandler, Averill Cook, Judy Licht, Colin O'Brien, Katie Tatro, and Alexis Van Uitert.

# Index

*Note:* Page numbers in *italic* indicate illustrations.

# Other Storey Titles You Will Enjoy

**The Basics of Western Riding** by Charlene Strickland. With clear photographs and illustrations, readers learn safe and effective horse-handling procedures and basic riding techniques. 144 pages. Paperback. ISBN 1-58017-030-7.

**Becoming an Effective Rider: Developing Your Mind and Body for Balance and Unity** by Cherry Hill. Riders learn to evaluate their own skills, plan a work session, get maximum use out of lesson time, set goals and achieve them, and protect themselves from injury. 192 pages. Paperback. ISBN 0-88266-688-6.

**Getting the Most from Riding Lessons** by Mike Smith. A reassuring introduction to riding, this book helps novice riders maximize the lesson experience, providing information about safety, horse behavior, basic riding exercises, and preparing for that first show. 160 pages. Paperback. ISBN 1-58017-082-X.

**101 Arena Exercises: A Ringside Guide for Horse and Rider** by Cherry Hill. Classic exercises and original patterns and drills are presented in a unique "read-and-ride" format. The book can be hung like a calendar or draped over the rail for easy reference. Exercises progress through skill levels for both English and Western riders. 224 pages. Paperback. ISBN 0-88266-316-X.

**101 Horsemanship & Equitation Patterns: A Western & English Ringside Guide for Practice and Show** by Cherry Hill. Full-page arena maps and careful instructions take you step-by-step through the most widely used patterns in the most popular classes of English and Western competition. The book's comb-bound format allows it to hang in the barn or draped over the rail for easy reference. 256 pages. Paperback ISBN 1-58017-159-1.

**Safe Horse, Safe Rider** by Jessie Haas. Beginning with understanding the horse and ending with competitions, this book includes chapters on horse body language, pastures, catching, and pages. Paperback. ISBN 0-88266-700-9.

**Teaching Safe Horsemanship: A Guide to English and Western Instruction** by Jan Dawson. Useful for anyone working with riders and horses, this essential guide covers becoming an effective, certified instructor, constructing lesson plans, teaching high-risk techniques. Explains protective release forms, insurance, and dealing with accidents or lawsuits. 160 pages. Hardcover. ISBN 0-88266-972-9.

**Your Pony, Your Horse: A Kid's Guide to Care & Enjoyment** by Cherry Hill. In a mature yet easy-to-read writing style, Cherry Hill offers kids ages 9 and up information on all aspects of horse care, plus equine activities for kids. 160 pages. Paperback. ISBN: 0-88266-908-7.

*These and other Storey Books are available at your bookstore, farm store, garden center, or directly from Storey Books, Schoolhouse Road, Pownal, Vermont 05261, or by calling 1-800-441-5700. Or visit our website at www.storeybooks.com.*